# US
# Error
# Note
# Encyclopedia

## 2nd Edition

Stephen M. Sullivan

# US Error Note Encyclopedia

Published by:    The US Currency Gallery
                 PO Box 73
                 Bonnerdale, AR 71933
                 www.capcurr.com

                 E-Mail: webmaster@capcurr.com


ISBN-13: 978-0-578-04520-7

**Reader Input**

Many years of research and in depth study have gone into the creation of this book. Hundreds of auction catalogs, press reports, dealers records (and dealers memories) and collectors have been consulted in an attempt to consolidate as much information as possible into a concise format. Many "closet" collections have remained locked away for the majority of the later half of the last century and some of them undoubtedly contain error notes that were not previously reported. The Grinnell sales of 1944 to 1947 spread the most significant error note holdings of that period across the globe and today (over 70 years later) many of these notes have not yet publicly resurfaced. These facts make it apparent that no text on this hobby can be complete. The author will be grateful to readers who notify him of any inaccuracy or important omission in this book.

# Table
# of Contents

Foreword.................................................................................................7

Acknowledgments.................................................................................9

Bibliography ......................................................................................11

Dedication..........................................................................................13

What is a Currency Error? ................................................................15

Why are Errors Collected?.................................................................18

Know Your Currency! ........................................................................20

Note Searching...................................................................................22

Paper Money Creation Overview........................................................24

Error Replacement Notes (Star Notes)...............................................50

Star Note Errors ................................................................................53

Grading ..............................................................................................54

Pricing ...............................................................................................58

Rarity Scale........................................................................................59

Alignment Problems ..........................................................................61
    Misaligned Face / Back ................................................................62
    Misaligned Overprint....................................................................74
    Overprint on Back ........................................................................92
    Inverted Overprint ......................................................................100
    Inverted Overprint on Back ........................................................116
    Inverted Back .............................................................................120

Cutting Errors ..................................................................................144
    MisCut Note ...............................................................................145

Engraving Errors.........................................................................................154
    Back Plate #1905 / 905........................................................................155
    Back Plate #7273 / 3273 ......................................................................156
    Back Plate #129....................................................................................157
    Fort Worth Plate Numbering Errors ....................................................158
        Face Plate 106................................................................................159
        Back Plate 295 ...............................................................................160
    Missing Plate Numbers.........................................................................161
    PCBLIC.................................................................................................162
    Date ReEngraved..................................................................................163
    Dropped "S" .........................................................................................164
    Signatures Reversed .............................................................................165
    Same Signatures ...................................................................................166

Extra Prints ...............................................................................................168
    Offset Printing .....................................................................................169
        Face to Back ..................................................................................172
        Back to Face ..................................................................................174
        Multiple .........................................................................................175
        Overprint .......................................................................................176
        Guide Roller Offset .......................................................................177
        Torn Note .......................................................................................178
    Multiple Impressions ...........................................................................190
        Standard Multiple Impressions......................................................192
        Partial Doubling ............................................................................193
        Loose Cylinder ..............................................................................194
        Multiple Impressions of Overprint ...............................................195
        Overprinting Machine Bounce ......................................................196
        Non-Standard Multiple Impressions..............................................197

Folds and Tears.........................................................................................216
    Gutter Fold ...........................................................................................217
    Unprinted Folds....................................................................................224
    Printed Folds & Tears ..........................................................................232

Inking Errors.............................................................................................244
    Ink Smear (Over Inked)........................................................................245
    Solvent Smear......................................................................................252
    Magnetic Ink Problems........................................................................258
    Under Inking........................................................................................265
        Underinking of Face and Back ......................................................266
        Insufficient Inking of Plate ...........................................................266
        Progressive Underinking ...............................................................267
        Underinking due to Insufficient Pressure .....................................268
        Underinking of Overprint ..............................................................269
    Wrong Ink Color ..................................................................................278

Missing Prints ............................................................................282
    Board Break ............................................................................283
    Obstructed Print........................................................................287
    Retained Obstruction................................................................295
    Missing Print (Complete) .......................................................304
        Missing Back (Blank Back)................................................305
        Missing Face.......................................................................310
        Missing Overprint..............................................................314

Overprint Errors.........................................................................320
    Identical Serial Numbers on Same Series Notes....................321
    Improperly Indexed Serial Numbers ......................................324
    Misaligned / Rolled Digit .......................................................326
    Mismatched Serial Numbers....................................................332
    Mismatched Prefix / Suffix Numbers .....................................350
    Mismatched Charter Numbers .................................................360
    Incorrect Geographical Designator..........................................364
    Inverted Digit ..........................................................................368
    Mismatched Block Font ..........................................................378
    District Designator Variance ..................................................382

    Paper Problems ........................................................................384
    Misplaced Watermark and/or Security Thread.........................385
    End of Roll Marker / Paper Splices.........................................390
    Thin / Thick Paper...................................................................398
    Lamination Errors....................................................................400

    Process Errors .........................................................................402
    Double Denominations.............................................................403
    Mixed Denominations .............................................................418
    Wrong Overprint .....................................................................423
    Test Note Errors ......................................................................428

Obstructed Plate .........................................................................430

Pre-Printed Stock ........................................................................432

Printed Scrap / Fragment............................................................434

Multiple Errors on Same Note ....................................................438

About the Author .........................................................................442

# Foreword

Although the first edition of this book was written 12 years ago, this version serves as a Silver Anniversary of sorts. Christmas 2009 will be the 25th anniversary of the day that my wife gave me my first error note, a Series 1957B $1 Silver Certificate with mismatched serial numbers (U[3|4]70).

My local coin (and a little currency) dealer told her that he thought I'd love it. The rest is history. I was immediately addicted and wanted to form a $1 error note collection consisting of an example of every type of error known. Within a month, I was at a small coin show in upstate New York asking every dealer with any currency to show me their errors. I found two more mismatched serial numbers at the show. They were both Series 1969 $1 FRN (F6[8|9]9) and they were just a few digits apart in serial numbers. They were both about the same grade, but one dealer wanted $40 for one and another wanted $90 for his example.

I studied each of them for a long time. I couldn't see why one would be more than twice the cost of the other, so I asked the higher priced dealer why. He shrugged his shoulders and said, "There ain't no reference on 'em. I'll match his price if you want it."

I bought the note from the lower priced dealer and went home happy.

I brought a spiral bound notebook with a green cover (I thought it was fitting) to the next show and started logging every error note that I found. This went on for several years. Soon dealers were asking me what I thought something was worth or how many of a particular error I'd seen.

We moved to Florida and I could find a coin show practically every weekend. Several dealers kept asking me when I was going to publish all of the stuff I had scrolled away in that (now ratty) green notebook.

I started working on the first edition of this book in 1995. With the help of a lot of people and the one very enthusiastic collector, I delivered the finished book to the International Paper Money Show in Memphis in June 1997.

A year later, I was sitting at my table at the same show, when I was approached by a gentleman cradling my book under his arm. He sat down and we started talking about all of the different error types. He asked me to help him assemble a set of every known error type from every denomination. To let me know he was serious, he purchased two large-sized double denominations that I had on consignment from a collector friend of mine.

Over the next six years, I assembled the landmark Taylor Family Collection of US Error currency. The collection was the largest and best of its kind. It eventually absorbed entire collections (including my own $1 Error Note collection that was second to none at the time.)

The Taylor Family Collection was auctioned off in 2005. It was (and still is) heralded as the best assemblage of error currency ever formed.

Because of this collection, I had the opportunity to handle virtually every type of error currency known. The collection also taught me more about errors that I had learned in the previous two decades.

This new knowledge enabled me to revise portions of the original version of this book and to add several more chapters.

Although this is only the second edition, this text has gone through more than a dozen revisions in the past 10 years.

While I no longer collect error currency (the Taylor Family Collection allowed me to handle practically everything as if it were my own), I still do a lot of research.

My other book, *Small Sized High Denomination Notes* was written after 10 years of research on the high denomination rarities that formed the Taylor Family Collection of $500 through $10,000 notes.

Thank you for reading.

Stephen M. Sullivan

# Acknowledgments

This book would have remained in its original format of a computerized database of error notes, boxes of catalogs, price lists and reference material and notebooks full of handwritten notes, prices, photographs and unanswered questions if it had not been for the assistance of many people.

I would like to thank the following people for their assistance:

Mike Abramson
Reecy Aresty
Billy Baeder
Willy Baeder
Ken Barr
Harry Bass
Carl Bombara
Gary Brown
Mike Byers
Lyn Chenn
Mike Crab, Jr.
Joel Cohen
Eric Danielson
Tom Denly
Norman Diamond
Richard Doty
Steve Edelson
Raphael Ellenbogen (deceased)
Kevin Foley
Dennis Forgue
Terry Fredricks
Donald Gilletti (deceased)
Aram Haroutunian
David Harper
Alan Herbert
Gene Hessler
Lowell C. Horwedel
Peter Huntoon
Peter Johnson
Harry Jones
Glen Jorde
A.M. Kagin (deceased)

Dr. Donald Kagin
Don Kelly
Laura A. Kessler
David Klein
David Koble
Doug Komm
Ed Kuzmar
Bob Kvederas
Bob Kvederas, Jr
George LaBarre
Fred Lake
J.L. Laws
Scott Lindquist
Jess Lipka
Ray Marrello
Robert McCurdy
Charles McGinnis
David Messner
Jon Morowitz
Douglas Murray
Dean Oakes
Michele Orzano
Alex Perakis
Lou Rasera
Brad Reed
Fred Rubenstein
Jeff Rubenstein
John Stone
Barry Schwartz
Randy K. Vogel
George Warner
Gordon White

Acknowledgments

I would like to extend a special "Thank You" to the following people:

Scott Kuzma for the countless hours spent providing me with additional scans and pricing guidance.

Lew Dufault for the additional scans and pricing help and his insightful theories on the creation of U.S. error currency.

Martin Gengerke for the use of his research database that is the foundation of my listings of Large Sized Error Notes.

Leonard Glazer and Allen Mincho of Currency Auctions of America, Inc. for the use of their cataloging records and photographs of US error currency.

Lyn Knight Currency auctions for the use of their cataloging records and photographs of US error currency.

I would also like to extend my gratitude to Frederick J. Bart for his insights on U.S. error currency and his willingness to share his extensive knowledge and insider information. Although many people think our books are competitors, they are really quite different and no library on U.S. currency can be considered complete without a copy of both.

Use of the Friedberg Numbering System is by license granted by the Coin & Currency Institute, Inc., publishers of Paper Money of the United States, copyright Arthur L. & Ira S. Friedberg, P.O. Box 1057, Clifton, NJ 07014.

# Bibliography

Consulted Periodicals:

    Bank Note Reporter, Krause Publications
    Numismatic News, Krause Publications
    Coin World, Amos Press
    Paper Money, Society of Paper Money Collectors
    The Numismatist, The ANA Library


ANA, *Selections from the Numismatists*, Whitman Publishing Co., Racine WI, 1960

Anton, William T. Jr, and Perlmutter, Morey, *The Albert A. Grinnell Collection of US Paper Money*, 1971. Originally catalogued by Barney Bluestone.

Azpiazu, Robert, The Collector's Guide to $1 FRN's Series 1963-2003A. Pip Printing, St, Augustine, Florida, 2005.

Bart, Frederick J., *Comprehensive Catalog of US Paper Money Errors*, various editions, 1994-

DeLorey, Tom and Reed, Fred, *Price Guide for the Collector of Modern US Paper Money Errors*, Amos Press, Sydney, OH, various editions, 1977 -

Donlon, William P., *US Large Size Paper Money 1861 to 1923*, A.M. & Don Kagin, Inc. Des Moines, Iowa, Sixth Edition, 1979

Friedberg, Robert, *Paper Money of the United States*, The Coin and Currency Institute, Inc., Clifton, NJ, various editions, 1978 -

Gengerke, Martin, *US Paper Money Records*, Martin Gengerke, New York, NY, various editions, 1984 -

Hessler, Gene, *The Comprehensive Catalog of US Paper Money*, 5th Edition. BNR Press, Port Clinton, Ohio. 1993.

Huntoon, Peter, *US Large Size National Bank Notes*, SPMC, 1995

Kelly, Don C., *National Bank Notes. A Guide With Prices*. 5th Ed. Paper Money Institute, Inc. Oxford, OH, 2006.

Bibliography

Krause, Chester L., and Lemke, Robert F., *Standard Catalog of US Paper Money*, various editions, 1987 -

Murray, Douglas D., *The Complete Catalog of United States Large Sized Star Notes 1910-1929.* 3$^{rd}$ Ed. Coin & Currency Institute, Clifton, NJ, 2007.

O'Donnell, Chuck, *The Standard Handbook of Modern US Paper Money*, Harry J. Forman, Inc., Philadelphia, PA, various editions, 1975-

Shafer, Neil, *A Guide Book of Modern US Currency*, Whitman Publishing Co., Racine, WI, various editions 1964 -

Schwartz, John & Lindquist, Scott, *Standard Guide to Small Sized U.S. Paper Money 1928 to Date*, 8$^{th}$ Ed. Krause Publications, Iola, WI, 2008.

Auction House Sales

Bowers & Merena - Irvine, California

Early American History Auctions - La Jolla, California

Heritage – Currency Auctions of America - Dallas, Texas

Ira & Larry Goldberg Coins & Collectibles – Beverly Hills, California

Lyn F. Knight - Overland Park, Kansas

R. M. Smythe - New York, New York

Spink America - New York, New York

Stack's - New York, New York

# Dedication

I would like to express my overwhelming gratitude and to dedicate this book to the following two people:

To my wife and best friend, Peggy Sue Sullivan. She changed my life more than a quarter of a century ago and to this day, she makes me want to be a better person. Everything good in my life is because of her in one way or the other.

To an anonymous collector who gave me the opportunity to put together the finest collection of error currency ever assembled. His friendship has shaped me in ways I never thought possible.

# What is a Currency Error?

A Currency Error is any note that does not meet the minimum quality standards of the Bureau of Engraving and Printing (BEP) but still somehow manages to escape being pulled during the many human and mechanical inspections. If the note is not perfect but would be considered "passable" by the inspectors, it is NOT classified as an error. With billions of notes being printed yearly, the quest for absolute perfection would be far too costly and time consuming. Many Series of notes are notorious for not being perfectly centered or for having off center Overprints that don't quite impair the face design. These problems are minor and common enough that they are not considered errors.

The BEP is the largest Securities Printer in the world. They produce a *product.* This product is circulated and traded worldwide and is a symbol of the economical stability and financial prowess of the United States of America. BEP workers take great pride in their workmanship and most do not like the fact that errors exist at all. Nearly one half of all US currency printed are $1 notes. A $1 note has an average life cycle of 18 months and will change hands an estimated 500 times during this period. An error on something as common as paper money is often very noticeable. In the past, the vast majority of error notes have been discovered by the non-collector. In the last decade, error note collecting has skyrocketed and there are collectors, dealers and bank tellers who are actively looking for that note that "just doesn't look right". Because of this, many of the modern errors can be easily found in uncirculated grades.

Currency that circulated during periods of financial uncertainty and economic depression in the US were passed on as quickly as possible. Even if the error was noticed, it was often more of a concern as to whether the grocer would accept it or not. If an error was discovered, it was often folded away in a wallet and displayed to friends as a conversation piece for many years because there were few coin dealers who could recognize the error as being marketable. Because of this, uncirculated examples of Large and early small sized currency are hard to find and often carry large premiums.

Paper Money was first issued in China and preceded the formation of The United States of America (USA) by over 1000 years. Government backed Paper Money was issued within the borders of what is now the USA since the late 1600's. It came in the form of Colonial, Continental, Territorials, State and Private Banks, Treasury Issued Interest Bearing Notes and even notes issued by the Confederate States of America. Many merchants also issued their own money (scrip) that could be used to purchase goods in their establishments. For nearly as long as US Paper money has existed, errors have been discovered and collected.

**State Bank Issue of 1862**
**Double Denomination**
**50 Cent Note with "Twenty Cents" printed on left side**

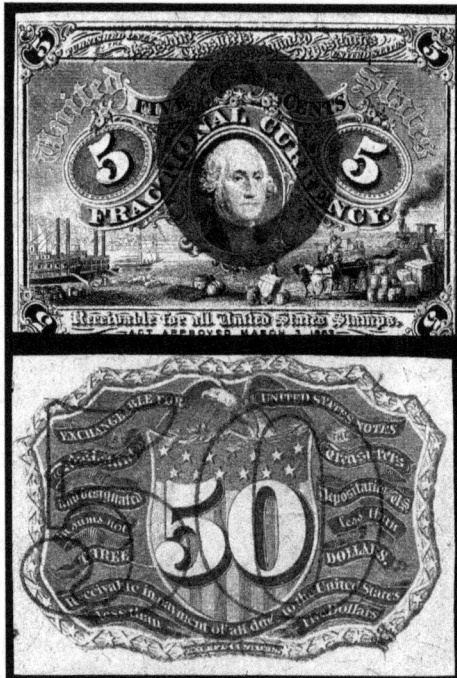

**Fractional Currency Issue**
**Double Denomination**
**5 Cent Face and 50 Cent Back**

**State Bank Issue of 1855**
**Inverted Back**

**Confederate States of America Issue of 1862**
**Inverted Back**

Although these notes were considered Legal Tender during their circulation period, the first official release of non interest bearing US Paper money did not occur until the issuance of the "Demand Notes" of 1861.

# Why are
# Errors Collected?

People collect error notes for many reasons. Some people collect them because of the rarity of even the most common errors. Although coin and currency enthusiasts see hundreds of these notes in many of the shows they attend and hundreds of them are illustrated in this book, considering that billions of notes are printed every year, there really are very few errors that ever reach circulation. An average of 6% of the notes produced are scrapped internally by the BEP The high quality of inspection processes at the BEP dictate that the number of errors that escape detection would have to be a small fraction of the total number of errors actually found internally. I have searched a minimum of 100 notes a week for 25 years. Considering that this number was a minimum and my search usually far exceeded that number, I estimate that I have examined over one hundred thousand notes from circulation during my collecting career and have discovered only three significant errors.

Some people enhance their collections by adding error notes with incredible "Eye Appeal". A note with an Inverted Overprint or a large Ink Smear is definitely very noticeable to even a non-collector. I receive e-mail from people all over the world who have a single note with a major error that was plucked from circulation many years ago and saved as a conversation piece.

Still others collect errors simply because these notes were never meant to reach circulation. BEP workers, like every other work force, take great pride in their work. Any error note is just that... an *error* and the workers hate for them to escape. They have very strict quality control. Their inspection processes continue to improve and much of the inspection is now enhanced with automated inspection equipment. The BEP won't be producing & releasing millions of these as some type of souvenir.

Some Currency Collectors spend their lives looking for the Superb Gem Crisp Uncirculated, "Best in Class" notes: perfect in every aspect. Others search for the *ugliest* (to the "best in class" collectors) notes that have as many mistakes as possible. Still others look for both. Many advanced collectors have a few "eye appealing" errors in their collections regardless of their collecting specialties.

The reasons that I started collecting Error notes are a combination of all of the above listed reasons. I will never forget my feeling of fascination as I held my first full, dark back to face offset (the first Paper Money Error that I had ever seen) or the excitement that rushed through my veins when my wife gave me my first one dollar note that had serial numbers that did not match for Christmas that same year. I was addicted! I also get very excited when I figure out how a particular error happened. Sharing this information with others and watching them "*see the light*" is an incredible feeling and probably the biggest reason whey I decided to put my personal research into this book format.

Regardless of why you collect error currency, I hope this book helps you to better understand how they are created and to appreciate their true rarity. I hope this book helps you to love error notes as much as I do.

**My First Error Note – A Christmas Present in 1984**

# Know
# Your Currency!

Some currency errors are very subtle. Many of these errors pass through circulation without ever being noticed. Others can be found in Dealers inventory or Junk Boxes without being labeled as an error. I once found a $1 Silver Certificate with an upside down "W" in the serial number (See *Inverted Digit* Chapter) in the junk box of a very prominent dealer.

Some of the more subtle currency errors that now command high prices are:

•      An upside down Star in the Serial Number of a replacement note.

•      Missing or misplaced plate numbers.

•      Reversed Signatures of Treasurer and Register.

•      Wrong color ink in Overprint.

•      A true rarity Error note is a type of Process Error that occurred when the Overprint of a Silver Certificate (Blue Overprint) was printed on a $5 Federal Reserve note (which should have had a green and Black Overprint). Federal Reserve Notes and Silver Certificates were both circulating at the same time during the discovery of this error. These notes may have passed through many hands (and probably even the hands of paper money collectors) but because this error is so subtle, it went undetected. Only two of these notes have been reported.

The most useful suggestion that I can give someone interested in Error Notes is to learn everything you can about US Paper Money. Know what it is supposed to look like. Know the major changes from series to series. Know how it is created and what can go wrong in these processes. This will make the minor (but sometimes truly rare) errors far more apparent.

**The Back Plate Number (129) is on the Wrong Side**

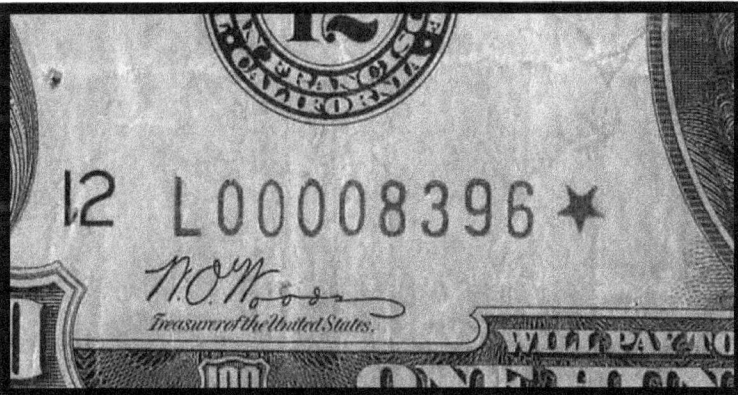

**The Star in The Serial Number is Upside Down**

# Note Searching - (Pack Searching)

The ultimate collecting experience for most Error Notes enthusiasts is to discover an error note in circulation. The increasing value of Error Notes has brought many dealers, collectors, bank tellers and anyone who handles large amounts of money into the note searching arena. Notes are carefully scrutinized for even the slightest problems that may increase their worth above face value.

What to look for when examining your notes:

- Face
  - Missing Portions
  - Lighter Portions
  - Plate Check Numbers
  - Margins - Misalignments or visible sheet numbers or alignment guides
  - Unprinted Wrinkles inside of the Design
  - Portion of Back Offset to Face
  - Correct Design for Series

- Overprint
  - Missing Digits or Seals
  - Mismatched Digits
  - Light or Darker Digits
  - Misaligned Digits
  - District Number and Serial No. Prefix Match
  - Colors are consistent and correct
  - Correct Design for Series
  - Alignmet to Face Printing

- Security Thread / Watermark
  - Missing
  - Wrong Denomination
  - Wrong Placement / Inverted
  - Stretched
  - Folded Over

- Back
  - Missing Portions
  - Lighter portions
  - Margins - Misalignments or visible sheet numbers or
    Back Plate Number
  - Unprinted Wrinkles inside of the design
  - Correct Design for Series

- Alignment of Back to Face
  - Misaligned / Skewed / Inverted

- Extra Paper Tab or Flags folded over

- Note Smaller or Larger than normal (due to miscutting)

- Paper too thick or too thin.

Examine notes in dealer inventories and junk boxes for the same things. Who knows? Maybe you will stumble across a 1985 $1 FRN with back plate 129 or an 1899 $1 Silver Certificate with face plate number 2985. Do these plate numbers mean anything to you? They should. Read the "Engraving Errors" chapter of this book and they will.

Good luck in the hunt!

# Paper Money Creation Overview

The question "How could this have happened?" is often asked when a Paper Money Error is examined. An understanding of how currency is created will add more insight into the things that can go wrong and how an error can occur.

The following chapter discusses each of the steps that are involved in the creation of US currency.

## Printing Plates

The printing plates are intaglio engraved. This means that the design is cut into the steel plate instead of being raised off from the plate. The ink fills the cuts of the incised plates and gives the design the 3D appearance once it is transferred to the sheet of notes. The ink is transferred by squeezing the paper between the printing plate and a rubber and cardboard covered impression roller under very high pressure. The paper is forced into the inked depressions of the plate.

The high pressure that is required to push the paper into the inked cutouts wears the plates down. Approximately one million impressions can be run from a single plate before it is considered too worn to produce a quality product.

These plates are engraved as a mirror image of the design intended for the note. The engravers have to envision each of the elements of the design in reverse. Several of the recorded engraving errors were probably the result of this difficult task.

A single master plate is used to create the printing plate cylinders so that each design is identical. Ever wonder why you can not find minor engraving differences in the portrait of your notes? The same engraved portrait of Grant that is used on the $50 note has been used for over 100 years.

# Ink

US currency is printed with special inks that are blended with top secret ingredients and are meant to be virtually impossible to duplicate. Four distinct colors are used to print modern Federal Reserve Notes. The backs are printed with green ink, the faces are black and the overprint is made up of green and black ink. The inks used in the overprinting are different shades than those of the back and the face and are easily distinguished from them. A black ink smear from the face printing that has part of the black ink from the overprint on top of it will easily show the overprint ink to be different.

Although the ink on US currency is supposed to be the same consistency and the same shades for all notes in a series, Federal Reserve Notes from Series 1928B and 1934 have two distinct colors of the Treasury Seal. The colors are classified as Dark Green and Light Green (or sometimes Yellow Green). These variations are not considered error notes.

Security features such as Magnetic ink and color changing ink are now being used on some US currency. Problems with this ink have made some very interesting errors (See *Inking Problems* Chapter).

# Paper

The paper used to create US currency is a blend of 75% cotton and 25% linen. It has a very high resistance to wear and can be washed and folded many times without being ruined.

The paper provides a home for several anti-counterfeiting techniques. Small blue and red threads are embedded into the paper at the pulp (liquid) stage. The paper is also dyed a distinctive cream color while in this liquid stage. Modern denominations of $5 to $100 currently have a plastic polymer thread running through them. The thread has the denomination and USA written across its length. 1996 and above Series $5 through $100 notes have a watermark of a scaled down portrait. The Security Thread and the Watermark are only visible when the note is held in front of a light source.

The paper is currently supplied exclusively by Crane Paper Company of Dalton Massachusetts. Crane has supplied paper for US currency since 1879. They have been the exclusive supplier since that time with the exception of some experimental notes printed for Series 1963 (See *Experimental Ink and Paper* section of this chapter).

**Wet and Dry Paper**

Intaglio printing required the paper to be wet in order to make it soft enough to be forced into the cuts of the printing plates to pick up the ink and hold it onto the paper while it dried. The paper was delivered from the manufacturer already dampened (*mill wet*). After the back printing, the ink needed to dry thoroughly before the face printing could be done. The drying of the ink also allowed the paper to dry and it was rewet prior to the face printing process.

The *wet print* process was difficult to work with. Strips of cardboard had to be inserted in between each sheet of notes as they came off from the printing press so that the ink would not transfer itself to the sheet above it. These strips had to be carefully inserted in the blank areas between and around the printed designs so that they would not smear the fresh ink.

A certain amount of shrinkage was expected as the paper dried but the shrinkage could vary between different lots of paper and different weather conditions (humidity) at the BEP printing facility. The exact measurements of the printed designs were very difficult to maintain. A variety of design sizes can be found when examining pre-1957 Series notes. The slight difference in size is normal and would not be considered an error.

After years of research by the BEP, the *dry print* method of Intaglio printing was introduced on Series 1957 $1 Silver Certificates (See *Sheet Sizes* section of this chapter for additional Information). Changes in the paper, ink and printing process were required to make this change a success.

## Experimental Ink, Paper and Presses

The paper and ink have been continuously refined and updated almost as long as the US has printed currency.

Much of the testing on these changes is done internally at the BEP but there has been a need to test the wear and durability of circulation on some of these changes. Since the $1 note is produced in greater quantity and sees more circulation than the other denominations, it is used as the test subject. The experimental notes are examined by the BEP for wear and durability after they have been circulated and returned to the Treasury from the Federal Reserve Banks.

**Series 1928A and 1928B**

1928A and 1928B Series $1 Silver Certificates were used to test a new type of paper. The linen content of the paper was modified to different proportions in two runs of notes.

**Series 1928-A & B Test Paper Notes**

| Feature | Starting Serial | Ending Serial |
|---|---|---|
| Varied Linen Content | X00000001B | X10728000B |
| Varied Linen Content | Y00000001B | Y10248000B |
| Control Series | Z00000001B | Z10248000B |

1928A and 1928B Series notes were intermixed within each of the Serial Number runs.

No Error Notes are known for this experimental issue.

**Series 1935**

1935 Series $1 Silver Certificates were used to test new paper and new paper finishes.

**Series 1935 Test Paper Notes**

| 1935 $1 SC | Starting Serial | Ending Serial |
|---|---|---|
| Special Paper Finish | A00000001B | A06180000B |
| Special Paper | B00000001B | B03300000B |
| Regular Control Series | C00000001B | C03300000B |

No Error Notes are known for this experimental issue.

## Series 1935A

1935A Series $1 Notes were used to test a special paper. The Special paper was marked with a large red "S" next to the Treasury Seal while the regular control paper was marked with a large red "R".

**Series 1935A Test Paper Notes**

| 1935A $1 SC | Starting Serial No. | Ending Serial No. |
|---|---|---|
| with red R (regular) | S70884001C | S72068000C |
| with red S (special) | S73884001C | S75068000C |

No Error Notes are known for this experimental issue.

**Series 1935F**

Series 1935F Notes from block B-J were used to test new equipment. These notes were meant to be destroyed after internal evaluations were performed but were released into circulation in an attempt to reduce BEP waste.

**Series 1935-F B-J Test Note**

| 1935F $1 SC | Starting Serial No. | Ending Serial No. |
|---|---|---|
| New Equipment Test | B71640001J | B72000000J |

No error notes are known for this experimental issue.

**Series 1963 Gilbert Test Paper**

Some series 1963 $1 Federal Reserve Notes were printed on paper that was supplied by the Gilbert Paper Company of Menasha, Wisconsin. This was the first time in nearly 100 years that US currency was printed on paper not supplied by Crane & Company of Dalton, Massachusetts.

**Gilbert Test Paper Note**

| Series 1963 $1 FRN | Staring Serial No. | Ending Serial No. |
|:---:|:---:|:---:|
| Gilbert Paper | C60800001A | C61440000A |

These notes were considered experimental and were used to test the quality and durability of paper supplied by a potential new source of currency paper.

The August of 1998 Report to Congressional Requestors entitled "Currency Paper Procurement" stated that Gilbert Paper Company did not submit an offer on additional paper procurements because they could not compete with Crane & Company's pricing.

No error notes have been reported from this run.

**Series 1977A Natick Test paper**

Some Series 1977A $1 and $10 Federal Reserve Notes were printed on experimental paper.

**Natick Test Paper Note**

| Denomination | Staring Serial No. | Ending Serial No. |
|---|---|---|
| $1 | E76800001H | E80640000H |
| $1 | E07052001★ | E07060000★ |
| $10 | E05772001★ | E05780000★ |

These notes were considered experimental but the results of this test were not reported by the BEP.

A small sampling of Inverted Overprint errors are known for the $1 E-H block.

**Web Notes**

The most recent experimental notes are printed on a continuous feed Web Press. They are commonly called Web Notes. The printing operation differs quite a bit from the conventional method of currency printing. The Web Press prints on a continuous feed roll of paper. The backs and the faces are printed in a single run.

**Web Note**

Web notes are easily identified because they do not have a Check Plate Position Letter on the upper left of the face or next to the Face Plate Number and the back plate number is above the Letter "E" in "ONE" instead of below it.

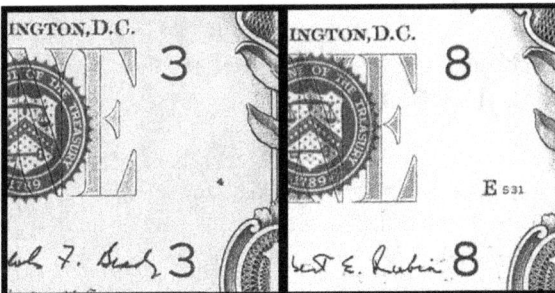

**Web Note          Regular Note**
**Face Plate Positioning and Appearance**

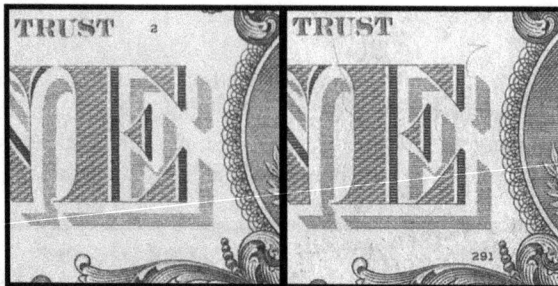

**Web Note          Regular Note**
**Back Plate Positioning and Appearance**

In 1992, the first Web notes were printed and released into circulation. All of these notes are $1 FRN's from Series 1988A, 1993 and 1995 (to date. Additional Web Notes that have had the back and face printings may be overprinted with a new series date). Web notes have had many different inking experiments performed on them and can be found with a variety of shades of black ink on the face of the notes. The Face design can make Washington's face appear light or dark and can make the ornate letters of the design appear to be completely filled of merely outlined.

In 1995, after three years and nearly 50 million dollars in expenses, the BEP announced that the Web Press was not cost effective and that the project was being discontinued.

**Note:** Errors on Web notes are very rare and highly sought after by error collectors and web note enthusiasts alike.

## Sheet Sizes and Plate Positions

US currency issued between 1861 and 1929 were larger (7-3/8" x 3-1/8") than the currency circulating today and are therefore often referred to as "Large" notes or "Large Sized" currency.

Large Sized currency was printed on 4 subject sheets. These sheets were printed on a flatbed printing press that worked by running a cylindrical plate counterclockwise over a wet sheet of paper that rested on a flat impression plate.

The Check Plate Positions for 4 Subject Plates are as follows:

| A | $1 |
|---|---|
| B | $1 |
| C | $1 |
| D | $1 |

**4 Subject Sheet**
**Face Plate Check Letters**

Check Plate Letters are found on the face of the note. They are often in the upper left hand portion of the note and they identify the position of any note in the full sheet it was printed on.

Plate Positions can be very important features when attempting to determine exactly how an error occurred. Small unprinted corner folds are unlikely on plate positions B and C on the 4 subject sheet shown above because the corners of the notes in these positions are attached to the notes directly above and below them. Almost every run of Mismatched Serial Numbers has happened on the same plate position. Each sheet would have only one incorrectly numbered note. There is only one known case of multiple mismatches from the same sheet (See *Mismatched Serial Numbers* Chapter).

Large Sized National Currency was often printed on multi-denominational sheets. Several denomination combinations are known to exist.

The Check Plate positions for 4 Subject Multi-Denominational Plates are shown in the following examples.

| A | $1 |
|---|---|
| B | $1 |
| C | $1 |
| A | $2 |

| A | $50 |
|---|---|
| B | $50 |
| A | $100 |
| B | $100 |

**Multi-Denominational 4 Subject Sheet**
**Face Plate Check Letter Examples**

35

Starting in 1929, with the introduction of small sized currency (Series 1928), notes were printed on 12 subject sheets. 12 Subject sheets were also printed on wet paper.

The Check Plate Positions for 12 Subject sheets are as follows:

| | |
|---|---|
| A | G |
| B | H |
| C | I |
| D | J |
| E | K |
| F | L |

**12 Subject Sheet**
**Face Plate Check Letters**

In 1953 the 18 subject sheets were introduced. The new sheet size was introduced in conjunction with the development of a quicker drying ink that would not offset onto the next sheet while it was drying. 18 subject sheets were also printed on wet paper.

| | | |
|---|---|---|
| A | G | M |
| B | H | N |
| C | I | O |
| D | J | P |
| E | K | Q |
| F | L | R |

**18 Subject Sheet**
**Face Plate Check Letters**

The 18 subject sheet was introduced as follows:

| Denom | Type | Series |
|---|---|---|
| $1 | SC | 1935D[1] |
| $2 | US | 1953 |
| $5 | FRN | 1950A |
| $5 | SC | 1953 |
| $5 | US | 1953 |
| $10 | FRN | 1950A |
| $10 | SC | 1953 |
| $20 | FRN | 1950A |
| $50 | FRN | 1950A |
| $100 | FRN | 1950A |

[1] - Series 1935D $1 Silver Certificates were printed on both 12 and 18 subject sheets.

The Rotary press with 32 subject plates was introduced in 1957. This press was designed to print with the Dry Intaglio method (dry sheets of paper printed with engraved plates).

The Check Plate Positions of 32 Subject Sheets are as follows:

| A1 | E1 | A3 | E3 |
|---|---|---|---|
| B1 | F1 | B3 | F3 |
| C1 | G1 | C3 | G3 |
| D1 | H1 | D3 | H3 |
| A2 | E2 | A4 | E4 |
| B2 | F2 | B4 | F4 |
| C2 | G2 | C4 | G4 |
| D2 | H2 | D4 | H4 |

**32 Subject Sheet Face Plate Check Letters**

The 32 subject sheet was introduced as follows:

| Denom | Type | Series |
|-------|------|--------|
| $1 | SC | 1957 |
| $2 | US | 1963 |
| $5 | FRN | 1963 |
| $5 | US | 1963 |
| $10 | FRN | 1963 |
| $20 | FRN | 1963 |
| $50 | FRN | 1963A |
| $100 | FRN | 1963A |
| $100 | US | 1966 |

The 32 subject rotary plates were used at the same time as the 18 subject presses over a period of 16 years. Series 1935F through 1935H $1 Silver Certificates were printed using the Wet Intaglio method at the same time that the Series 1957 through 1957B $1 Silver Certificates were printed using the Dry Intaglio Method.

The order of printing $1 SC's was as follows:

| Series | Method / Sheet Size |
|--------|---------------------|
| 1957 | Dry Intaglio / 32 subject sheets |
| 1935F | Wet Intaglio / 18 subject sheets |
| 1957A | Dry Intaglio / 32 subject sheets |
| 1935G w/o Motto | Wet Intaglio / 18 subject sheets |
| 1935G with Motto[1] | Wet Intaglio / 18 subject sheets |
| 1957B | Dry Intaglio / 32 subject sheets |
| 1935H | Wet Intaglio / 18 subject sheets |

[1] - The Motto "IN GOD WE TRUST" was added to the engraved back plates of all denominations of notes. (See BACK PRINTING section for more details.)

# Plate Numbers

The BEP's rotary presses are equipped with different types of printing cylinders that can accommodate 1, 2 or 4 printing plates. Consecutive notes printed the single plate press will have plate numbers that are all the same. Notes printed on the 2 plate press will have plate numbers that duplicate every other note and notes printed on the 4 plate press will have duplicate plate numbers every 5th note. These presses were used simultaneously so it is not uncommon to find a group of consecutively Serial Numbered notes that have a back plate number all the same (if the backs were printed on the 1 Plate setup) while the face plate number is duplicated every 5th note (if the faces were printed on the 4 Plate setup) or any other combination of plate numbers that can come from this setup.

This production anomaly could result in a very unusual run of plate errors. It is possible to find a consecutively numbered run of notes that had a partial offset of back to face every other note and a partial offset of face to back every fourth note.

The 4 plate presses are used mainly to print $1 Federal Reserve notes. Much of the higher denominations are printed on the 1 and 2 plate presses.

# Order of Printing

Many questions have arisen as to how some consecutive errors get more dramatic as the Serial Numbers increase and some get more dramatic as the Serial Numbers decrease. To better understand this, an understanding of the printing process is required.

The backs of notes are printed first. The first sheet to enter the back printing press will be the sheet at the top of a pallet of 20,000 sheets. This sheet becomes the bottom sheet of the pallet of printing notes.

The pallets are allowed to dry for a minimum of 24 hours and then the sheets must be flipped over to allow the unprinted side to receive the face printing.

The first sheet to enter the face printing press will be the sheet at the top of the pallet of 20,000 sheets. This sheet becomes the bottom sheet of the pallet of printing notes. Because the Pallet was flipped over after the back printing was allowed to dry, the first sheet to get the face printing is also the first sheet that received the back printing

The pallets are allowed to dry for another 24 hours and then can receive the Overprinting. Since the sheets are already positioned face up, and the Overprint is applied to the face, the pallets do not need to be flipped over for this process.

The Serial Numbers are applied to the notes in decreasing order. The highest Serial Number is applied to the note at the top of the pallet so that the Serial Numbers will increase though the stack of notes after they have gone though the Overprinting Process. This process makes the sheet with the lowest Serial number be the same sheet that had the first back and face printings.

## Process Considerations

Some consecutive errors are known that do not follow these guidelines. Some sheets that are found to contain errors are pulled from the production run before they progress to the next stage of printing. A missed first impression (Dark) Offset (transfer of ink meant for one side of the note to the other) can have consecutive notes that do not have any trace of the offset error because the other error sheets were pulled during production.

The printed sheets are moved from the printing press to the pallets manually. Some sheets are taken off from the pallets at different intervals of the printing process and inspected for errors. These sheets are returned to the pallets but are often placed out of order. This can make consecutive errors also appear to be unexplainable.

**Author's Note:** I once examined a 3 note set of Offsets that had the Serial Number of the first (darkest) impression between the Serial Numbers of the second and third impressions.

## Back Printing Details

The Backs of US currency printed by the BEP have always been printed first. In 1863 correspondence between the Treasury and the National Banknote Company and the American Banknote Company (private security printers used to print all aspects of US currency except for the overprinting) made it apparent that these private companies were printing the backs and faces in no particular order. Further correspondence during this time frame acknowledged that a $1 "Blank back" note was possibly the result of such activities. This $1 note has not resurfaced in over 130 years.

The backs of US currency have always been smaller than the faces. This is done to make the alignment of faces and the backs easier. As a rule, as long as the back design falls within the design of the face, it is considered properly aligned.

If the backs and faces were exactly the same size, a fraction of an inch of misalignment would be very apparent.

Near the end of 1952, some of the notes being printed had the backs narrowed by 1/16 of an inch.

The backs of the following notes were affected:

| Denomination | Type | Series |
|:---:|:---:|:---:|
| $1 | SC | 1935D |
| $5 | SC | 1934D |
| $5 | US | 1928F |
| $10 | SC | 1934D |
| $10 | FRN | 1950 |

This change was in conjunction with the changeover from a 12 subject sheet to an 18 subject sheet. The back designs were made smaller because there was concern that the larger sheets would make the alignment of the face and back more difficult. The change in the design size also coincided with the BEP working with several US and European printing press manufacturers in an attempt to develop a suitable "dry print" press. The back and face designs were intentionally made oversized for the "wet print" process because a small amount of shrinkage was expected as the paper dried. There has been speculation that the new back sizes were created in anticipation of the experiments that would be run on the presses although the actual change over to the "dry print" process did not occur until the later part of 1957.

The Motto "IN GOD WE TRUST" was added to the back of the $1 Silver Certificate in the middle of Series 1935G. Some notes from this Series were printed with the motto and some were not. All subsequent Series bear this motto.

The Serial Numbering Sequence for this Series is as follows:

| 1935G $1 SC | Staring Serial No. | Ending Serial No. |
|:---:|:---:|:---:|
| without Motto | B 54000001 J | D 48960000 J |
| with Motto | D 48960001 J | D 80280000 J |

Replacement (Star) note Serial Numbers are not listed due to the fact that the exact number of Star notes that were required to complete these runs is not known. Star note runs of these notes were printed but not all of the Series were released into circulation. Recorded High and Low Serial Numbers constantly change as new discoveries are made.

Aside from the $1 Silver Certificates, the Motto was introduced on the following denominations:

| Denomination | Type | Series |
|:---:|:---:|:---:|
| $2 | US | 1963 |
| $5 | US | 1963 |
| $5 | FRN | 1963 |
| $10 | FRN | 1963 |
| $20 | FRN | 1963 |
| $50 | FRN | 1963A |
| $100 | FRN | 1963A |

## Face Printing Details

After freshly printed backs are allowed to dry for a minimum of 24 hours, the pallets are moved from the drying rooms into a press room that is setup for face printing.

The face printing setup is identical to that of the back printing with one exception. After the faces are printed, the 32 subject sheets are automatically split into two 16 subject sheets for easier inspection. The smaller sheets pass through inspection stations so that the face design can be inspected. They are then mechanically flipped over as they continue forward so that a second inspection station can verify the back printings. This process is automated now but prior to 1981, the 32 subject sheets were being cut and inspected manually.

Some notes were printed with the engraved signatures of the Treasurer and Secretary of the Treasury or Register while other notes had these signatures placed on the note in the Overprinting process.

In 1861, several million "Demand Notes" were authorized to be printed. In order for these notes to become Legal Tender, the signatures of the Register and the Treasurer were to be hand signed on each of the notes. It quickly became apparent that it would be an impossible task for these two men to sign the millions of notes that were being printed so Congress accepted the idea that people could be designated to sign for each of these officials. New plates were engraved with the words "for the" placed beside the titles of the Register and the Treasurer to make the other signatures legal. In the interim, the words "for the" were handwritten on some of the notes. These notes are rare but are not errors.

This solution proved to be costly and the signatures of unknown people were easily counterfeited. Series 1862 US Notes had the signatures of the officials engraved on the face plates. This practice was continued for all Large Sized currency and through Series 1934 small sized currency. Plate engraving was a lengthy process so the signatures and Series Date were moved to the Overprinting process so that currency production would not be delayed during the wait for new face plates.

The signatures and Series Date were moved to the Overprinting process.

They were introduced as follows:

| Denomination | Type | Series |
|:---:|:---:|:---:|
| $1 | SC | 1935 |
| $2 | US | 1953 |
| $5 | US | 1953 |
| $5 | SC | 1953 |
| $5 | FRN | 1950 |
| $10 | SC | 1953 |
| $10 | FRN | 1950 |
| $20 | FRN | 1950 |
| $50 | FRN | 1950 |
| $100 | FRN | 1950 |

Modern US currency has the Signatures and Series Date printed on the face plates once again.

The engraved plates were introduced as follows:

| Denomination | Type | Series |
|:---:|:---:|:---:|
| $1 | FRN | 1963B |
| $5 | FRN | 1969 |
| $10 | FRN | 1969 |
| $20 | FRN | 1969 |
| $50 | FRN | 1969 |
| $100 | US | 1966 |
| $100 | FRN | 1969 |

## Back and Face Production Details

The backs and faces are printed by passing a sheet of paper between a steel print cylinder and a rubber covered impression cylinder under extreme pressure.

Ink is applied (charged) to the entire printing plate from a roller attached to an inking fountain. The surface is then wiped clean with a cloth wiper. Ink is left in the incised cuts of the engraved plate and will be picked up by the sheet of paper when the paper is press between the cylinders. After the cylinder is wiped, it is polished with a rotating polisher to ensure that all of the excess ink is removed. The printing plate is recharged for every printing.

During the back and face printing process, the sheets are moved and aligned with the help of a conveyor system, mechanical fingers and guides, suction cups and jets of air.

The sheets are fed into the printing cylinders from bottom to top. Once they exit that printing operation, they can be moved laterally to other conveyors with the help of alignment wheels and guides. These guides are the largest contributor to corner folds that may result in Fold and Tear errors (See *Folds and Tears* Chapter).

The alignment wheels can also smear the fresh ink if the sheet is not properly aligned when it passes under them.

Malfunctioning alignment guides and improperly position full sheets of notes lead to most of the known Alignment Errors.

## Mules

Early in the production of small sized currency, face and back plate numbers were doubled in size (macro) due to the difficulty the inspectors had in seeing these numbers on the smaller printed sheets. Some plates bearing the older, smaller plate numbers (micro) were still usable and continued to be utilized. When the back of a note bears one size plate number and the face of the note bears the other, the note is called a *mule*.

**Mule with Micro Face Plate and Macro Back Plate**

44

The Change Over to Larger Plate Numbers was introduced as follows:

| Denomination | Type | Series |
|:---:|:---:|:---:|
| $1 | SC | 1935A |
| $2 | US | 1934A |
| $5 | SC | 1934A |
| $5 | FRN | 1934A |
| $10 | SC | 1934A |
| $10 | FRN | 1934A |
| $20 | FRN | 1934A |
| $50 | FRN | 1934A |
| $100 | FRN | 1934A |

Mules are not errors but are still sought after by collectors.

The one mule type that would be considered an error would be a note that should have been printed with a back plate containing the motto "IN GOD WE TRUST" but was printed with an older plate that did not have the motto.

**Author's Note:** No genuine examples of this error are known to exist. All examined claims of this error were found to have been altered by removing the motto.

## Overprinting Details

Overprinting is often referred to as the 3rd printing but this can be misleading. Overprinting is defined as anything that is printed on the notes after the back and face prints are completed. This is currently the Serial Numbers, Treasury Seal and District Seal and numbers. In the past, the overprint included the word "HAWAII" printed twice on the face and once on the back, National Bank information, Treasurer and Registers signatures and Bank Official signatures and printings on the face and back of some fractional currency. Some of these processes required a 4th and 5th printing.

The Serial Numbers that are printed in the overprinting process do not index upwardly Starting at A00000001A and Ending with A00020000A in the First Plate position of the first complete run of notes. Instead, they index downwardly so that the last sheet to receive the overprint will be the lowest number and also be the top sheet of the pallet. (See *Printing Processes Section* of this chapter). The Serial Numbers are reset for each run of 20,000 sheets.

$1 Series 1935D and 1935E used a multiple overprinting process that printed the Blue Overprint (Seal and Serial Numbers) and the Black Overprint (Series and Signatures) separately.

Any Multiple colored print on US currency has always been done separately but in the case of the overprinting, the two colors were thought to have been added by the same piece of equipment. Modern Federal Reserve Notes have the Treasury Seal and Serial Numbers printed with green ink at the beginning of the Overprinting process and seconds later the District Seal and District Numbers are added with black ink. Several errors on Series 1935D and 1935E $1 Silver Certificates question this process. Notes have been discovered with the Blue portion of the Overprint correctly positioned while the black portion was misaligned and the Black portion correctly positioned while the Blue portion has been misaligned. These two Series have also given birth to the only reported finds (on small sized Silver Certificates) with inversions of one color but not the other. All observed instances of these errors have had a **G** for the suffix of the Serial Number. BEP reports of currency release dates show that the **G** suffix letter was used in the earliest runs of these series. It seems nearly impossible for these errors to occur if both colored portions of the overprint were printed on the same machine.

## New Treasury Seal in Overprint

A new Treasury Seal was introduced that had the Latin inscription translated into English.

**Old Style Seal**          **New Style Seal**

The New Seal was introduced as follows:

| Denomination | Type | Series |
| --- | --- | --- |
| $1 | FRN | 1969 |
| $2 | FRN | 1976 |
| $5 | FRN | 1969 |
| $10 | FRN | 1969 |
| $20 | FRN | 1969 |
| $50 | FRN | 1969 |
| $100 | US | 1966 |
| $100 | FRN | 1969 |

Series 1963A notes were being printed for all of the Federal Reserve Notes except the $2 denomination during this change. While none have ever been reported, it is possible that the Latin Seal was inadvertently printed on the newer notes or that the English Seal was printed on the older notes.

# COPE-PAK

COPE-PAK is an acronym for Currency Overprinting and Processing Equipment and Packaging. These machines apply the green and black overprints to half sheets of currency.

Immediately after the Overprints are put on the notes, the margins of the half sheets are trimmed to a standard size and stacks of 100 are first cut into horizontal pairs (two notes, side by side) and then into individual notes. Stacks of 100 of these individual notes are then banded together for packaging.

The sheets of notes are moved through the overprinting equipment on a conveyor system that utilizes a series of mechanical fingers, guides, suction cups and jets of air. The COPE-PAK machine has full electronic error detection and is supposed to shut the press down when errors are found.

Prior to the introduction of the COPE-PAK machines in 1972, Overprinting, cutting and packaging were separate operations.

## Design Alignments

The back, face and overprints of a note are all designed to be in a specific place on each note. They also have a relationship to each other. When held up to a light source so that the back, face and overprint are all visible, the back design should fall within the borders of the face design and the overprint should not impair any part of the face design.

Problems with any of these printing can create some very eye appealing errors (See *Alignment Errors* Chapter).

## Inspection Details

Each step in the currency making process is supplemented with at least one inspection. Today's printings have complete electronic inspections with redundant human inspections. Individual notes that are found to be substandard are marked with a red inspectors crayon and/or a rejection sticker. These stickers are placed in the lower right hand corner of the affected notes. The full sheet is allowed to continue through the printing process with the intention that the marked note will be pulled after the sheets are cut into individual notes. Some of the electronic equipment in the COPE-PAK machines looks for these rejection stickers. Prior to the introduction of the electronic inspection equipment, the final inspectors searched each pack of 100 notes for these marked notes.

**Error Note Marked With Rejection Sticker**

**Error Note Marked With Inspectors Red Crayon**

## Fort Worth Notes

As the annual production of US currency approached 6 billion notes, it became apparent that the BEP facility in Washington DC was not large enough to accommodate the requirement for an ever increasing number of notes.

In 1991, the BEP opened its western facility in Fort Worth Texas. Notes printed at the Fort Worth plant differ slightly from the notes printed in Washington DC. They have the FW prefix before the Lower left Check Plate number on the face of a note and a larger back plate number.

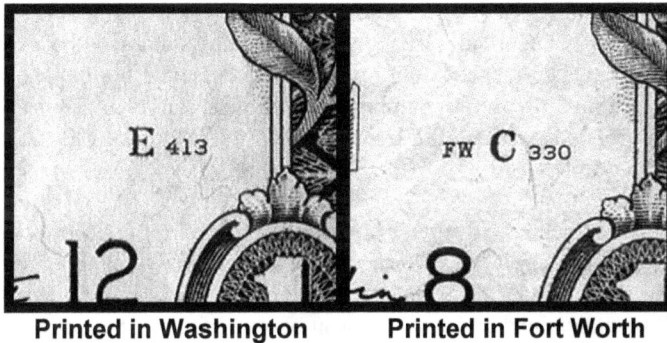

**Printed in Washington        Printed in Fort Worth**

Currently the market does not see a price difference between errors on notes that are printed in Washington DC or in the Forth Worth facility.

## Summary

The creation of US paper money is not an easy task. There are dozens of steps that rely on human responses, the reliability of electronic inspection equipment and a continuous flow of events in a specific order. Billions of new notes are created every year and breakdowns have occurred at every point possible. Problems can arise in any of the steps outlined in this chapter and the first major redesign of US Currency (starting with Series 1996 $100 Federal Reserve Notes) in 80 years has given birth to the possibility of errors never before encountered.

# Error Replacement Notes (Stars)

When defective notes are found internally at the BEP, they are removed and destroyed. This can make the accounting process very difficult because some of the stacks of notes that are supposed to contain 100 notes will be short due to the removal of the errors. It would be very time consuming and costly to record the shortages so a method of replacing the spoilage had to be developed.

Early methods of replacing error notes involved the substitution with notes bearing previously recorded serial numbers, rubber stamping the exact same serial number of the erroneous note on another note from a stockpile of notes preprinted without the serial numbers and rubber stamping the same serial number on error notes where the error involved the Overprint and the note was deemed salvageable.

In 1910, a new method of replacing errors was developed. Series 1899 notes were printed with a Star symbol as the Prefix to the Serial Numbers. These notes were otherwise identical to other notes in the same series. An accurate count could still be maintained and a comparison between the number of spoiled notes and the expended "Star" notes would greatly simply internal auditing and accounting requirements. The "Star" Note system quickly proved effective and is still in use today.

Federal Reserve Notes and Federal Reserve Bank Notes use the star as the suffix of their serial Numbers because the Prefix letter is used to identify the Federal Reserve District that the note was printed for. The other types of notes that utilize the "Star" system replace their Prefix letter with the star.

**Replacement Note with Star as Suffix**

**Replacement Note with Star as Prefix**

The Star was used in earlier (pre-1899) series along with a variety of other symbols to designate the end of the serial number. This was an anti-counterfeiting technique used in an attempt to eliminate the possibility that a batch of notes could be printed with the same serial numbers (as overprinting was generally done on the same printing plates as the face designs in early counterfeiting practices). Other characters could be added to make two notes with the same serial numbers appear to be different and to continue to fool merchants once the serial number of known counterfeits were publicized.

## 100 Millionth Note in Block

Star Notes are also used to Replace the 100 millionth note in a run. The notes are stacked in piles of 100 so the number printed must be a multiple of 100 to maintain a proper count.

**100 Millionth Note in Block**

The numbering cogs in the overprinting presses were only capable of printing 8 digits and the prefix and suffix letters. The 9th digit in this note dictated that the serial number had to be hand set. This is no longer the case with the COPE-PAK machines.

The 100 millionth note was printed with Serial Number 100 000 000 for several series of notes.

**Reported Examples**

| Denom. | Type | Series | Fr No. | Serial No. |
|---|---|---|---|---|
| $1 | SC | 1899 | Fr 226 | 100000000 |
| $1 | SC | 1899 | Fr 232 | M100000000M |
| $1 | SC | 1899 | Fr 232 | N100000000N |
| $1 | SC | 1899 | Fr 233 | R100000000R |
| $1 | SC | 1899 | Fr 235 | H100000000A |
| $1 | SC | 1923 | Fr 237 | N100000000D |
| $1 | SC | 1928A | Fr 1601 | C100000000B |
| $1 | SC | 1928B | Fr 1602 | G100000000B |
| $1 | SC | 1934 | Fr 1606 | A100000000A |
| $1 | SC | 1934 | Fr 1606 | B100000000A |
| $1 | SC | 1934 | Fr 1606 | F100000000A |
| $2 | US | 1917 | Fr 58 | A100000000A |
| $5 | FRN | 1918 | Fr 871 | G100000000A |

When this practice was discontinued for 1935 and later Series, the need for the 100th note in the final run dictated that a star note be used in its place.

Modern Currency Overprint Equipment only allows for the printing of 8 digits between the Prefix and the Suffix letters. It was rumored that the 100 millionth note was still printed but that it contained 8 zeros in the serial number. This note was removed and replaced with a star note. The BEP has denied that this process is followed, but the discovery of a Series 1963 $1 Federal Reserve Note bearing Serial Number A00000000A is proof enough for the collecting community that the BEP continued to print a note that was supposed to be replaced with the Star note.

Because Star Notes are used primarily as replacement notes it should be rare to find long consecutive runs of these notes, however, the BEP routinely releases packs of 100 Star Notes into circulation when the stockpiled notes are not being depleted quickly enough and a new Series is printed.

# Star Note Errors

No Special precautions or inspection processes are performed on Star Notes. Star notes are printed in exactly the same manner as regular notes. In fact, it is not known if the final product will be a regular note or a star note during the back and face printings. This is not determined until the Overprinting process.

Because Star notes are used to replace errors, an error on a Star is a prized acquisition.

## Large Sized Currency

Large Sized Star note errors are very rare.

### Known Examples

| Denom. | Type | Date | Fr No. | Serial No. | Error |
|---|---|---|---|---|
| $1 | SC | 1899 | Fr 230 | ★2211584B | Inverted Back |
| $1 | SC | 1899 | Fr 232 | ★4183779B | Inverted Back |
| $1 | SC | 1899 | Fr 234 | ★12196154B | Inverted Back |
| $5 | SC | 1899 | Fr 274 | ★86518B | Inverted Back |
| $1 | LT | 1917 | Fr 36 | ★3594132B | Butterfly Fold |
| $1 | LT | 1917 | Fr 37 | ★8208892B | Gutter Fold |
| $1 | LT | 1923 | Fr 40 | ★4411D | Gutter Fold |
| $1 | LT | 1923 | Fr 40 | ★4412D | Gutter Fold |
| $1 | LT | 1923 | Fr 40 | ★141223D | Gutter Fold |
| $1 | SC | 1923 | Fr 237 | ★1559176D | Inverted Back |
| $1 | SC | 1923 | Fr 237 | ★15182952D | Inverted Back |
| $1 | SC | 1923 | Fr 238 | ★20813224D | Inverted Back |
| $2 | LT | 1917 | Fr 57 | ★611598B | Inverted Back |
| $2 | LT | 1917 | Fr 60 | ★2828827B | Inverted Back |
| $2 | LT | 1917 | Fr 60 | ★3351684B | Inverted Back |
| $5 | LT | 1907 | Fr 85 | ★358663B | Inverted Back |
| $5 | LT | 1907 | Fr 91 | ★3174735B | "PCBLIC" Engraving |
| $5 US | | 1907 | Fr 91 | ★3201018B | "PCBLIC" Engraving |
| $5 | FRN | 1914 | | C54997★ | Misaligned Back |
| $5 | FRN | 1914 | Fr 870 | G430965★ | Gutter Fold |
| $10 | FRN | 1914 | Fr 911c | B1337007★ | Misaligned OP |
| $10 | FRN | 1914 | Fr 930 | G422004★ | Butterfly Fold |
| $20 | GC | 1906 | Fr 1185 | ★125992B | Inverted Back |

# Grading

The condition (grade) of an error note reflects directly upon the value of that note. The better the condition, the higher the value. Many characteristics can affect the grade of US paper money. Folds, amounts of wear, crispness, stains, shininess are just a few things that can change the desirability (and therefore the price) of a note.

This book lists the retail prices of error notes for three of the more common grades when this pricing information is available.

Several Third-Party Grading houses have sprung up since the first edition of this book. These services use a numeric grading system similar to that of Coin grading services, but the grades assigned by these services has been seen to vary widely. Many people still disagree on many subtleties when attempting to grade a note.

Nearly every Numismatic reference book defines grading standards differently. The following guidelines are compilations of grading standards that are most commonly accepted among dealers and buyers of paper money. These are only guidelines. The grades assigned to some of the rare and unique notes in this reference will not all abide by these guidelines. Many of the listed grades were taken from auction catalogs and dealer records.

## Crisp Uncirculated (CU) - Sometimes referred to as NEW

No Folds but may have wrinkle that does not extend from edge to edge
No Rounded Corners
No Stains or Faded Colors

## About Uncirculated (AU)

Minor Teller or Machine Handling evident
Up to 1 Light Fold
Very Slightly rounded corners
Note retains original Shininess

## Extremely Fine (EF or XF)

Up to 3 light folds
Corners rounding more pronounced
Paper is bright and fairly clean
Note retains original shininess
Embossing is still evident

## Very Fine (VF)

Several Folds and Wrinkles
No Tears
Slightly Dirty
Still fairly Crisp
Ink is slightly Faded
Note may appear flat with no embossing visible

## Fine (F)

Wear along edges and corners
Tears in margins that do not impair design
Paper may be dirty
Staple Holes
Note Still retains some of its rigidness
Colors are easily identifiable.

## Very Good (VG)

Severely Rounded corners.
Tears that extend into the Design
Staining
Discoloration
Tears or Holes along folds
No portion of Note may be missing

## Low Grades

Notes that grade lower than the above guidelines can also be graded Good (G), Fair (FA), and Poor (PR).

A note that is assigned a grade of Good or lower is usually considered non-collectable. This is not the case with error notes. As all errors are considered rare, even a note in Good condition would be a valuable asset to most error note collections. Who among us would turn away from a double denomination or a large inverted back star note because it is torn or missing a large portion of a corner?

## Superb, Gem and Choice Grades

These descriptors refer to the notes that are at the very top of the grade. Centering of the back, face and overprint is often much better than normal on notes of these grades. These grades are not used in this reference work.

## Plus and Minus and *About* Grades

Often a note will not quite meet the standards of one grade but seem to exceed those of the next lower grade. Third party Grading Services has taken care of this problem with the assignment of numbers associated with different levels of each grade. Notes not graded by a third party grading service are often handled with the assignment of a plus or minus sign to the grade. If the Note is not quite VF but definitely better than an F grade, it will grade VF-. If a Note is a Solid F but has brighter colors or better centering than the average FINE note it may grade an F+ or F/VF. This note will also sometimes be graded About Very Fine (AVF).

## Split Grades:  Face and Back grade differently.

The face and back of a note are usually not graded separately. The notes grade is a compilation of the face, back and overprint. While attempting to price a note that has been "Split Graded" assign the grade to the plus side of the lower of the two grades.

## More Grading Considerations

The Error does not affect the grade of the note. Many errors are created when the paper folds, wrinkles or tears. Any of the items that are a result of the error must be ignored when grading an error note.

*Foxing* is light brown or yellow stain on a note that is the result of a mold. The mold usually eats away the paper and is found on both sides of the note. The paper inside the stain is often very thin.

Bank Tellers use a rubber stamp to mark banded packs of currency after they are counted. These stamps (called Teller Stamps) often mark the top note in the banded pack with a portion of the inked stamp design. Portions of these stamps are visible on many modern CU notes and these marks should be identified with the Grade of the note.

Bank employees also use a *Magic Marker* to identify notes that are distributed through their Automatic Teller Machines. Many modern CU high denomination ($20 and higher) have a permanent ink mark along the top margin. This mark has been seen in a variety of colors and is usually no more than 1/2" in length. Notes bearing these *ATM marks* should have the mark identified with the grade of the note.

Teller Stamps and ATM Marks are imperfections and do decrease the value of a note.

# Pricing

Prices on virtually everything are determined by what people are willing to pay to obtain the item and are then maintained and adjusted by the trends (average) that people have continued to pay for similar items.

The prices in this book are an average of prices realized in Dealer sales, Auctions, and Private transactions. They should be used as a guideline of retail prices only. A wide range of prices can be found for similar error notes and more collectors and dealers are flooding the market place each day. Prices will continue to change as quickly as the supply and demand changes.

Rarity does not always play a major factor when pricing an error note. A unique Engraving error that involves the engraving of the signatures of the Treasurer of the United States twice on the face of a note is not as visually appealing as a massive Foldover error with a huge portion of the face and overprint printed on the back of the note. Prices often reflect the eye-appeal aspect of the error.

# Rarity Scale

I've adopted the 9 point scale developed by Dr. Frederick J. Bart in 1995.

Each error category is assigned a rarity number with an R1 being the most common and an R9 being the rarest.

Assigning a rarity rating to error notes with similar errors is not completely accurate because an Inverted Overprint on a note printed between 1976 and 1978 is less rare than on a note printed in 1995 (because hundreds of Inverted Overprints were discovered between 1976 and 1978 while only a handful are known on Series 1995 notes). The same can be said about the G5[5|4]4 Mismatched Serial Numbered $1 Silver Certificate. 10,000 of these notes were released and the quick discovery of the error made national headlines and many were saved in very high grades. One of these notes will not have the same rarity rating as the D[4|3]23 Mismatched Serial Numbered $1 Federal Reserve note.

Because the majority of error note collectors assemble collections of a note from each category, this type of rarity assignment seems to work best, but pricing considerations should be noted within each category.

# Alignment Errors

The back, face and overprints of a note are all designed to be in a specific place on each note. They also have a relationship to each other. When held up to a light so that both the face and back designs are visible, the back design should be completely within the borders of the face design. The overprint should not impair any part of the face design.

The back and face printing plates have alignment tabs engraved on them to aide the production workers in keeping the full sheets properly oriented. Mechanical guides and fingers are used to ensure that the sheets are kept in place during the overprint process.

A note that has one or two of the three major design elements (back, face, and overprint) out of their proper orientation with respect to each other is classified in the Alignment Error family.

Although a note that has its back, face and Overprint all aligned properly to each other but all three elements are out of alignment with the cut of the final note is a type of *cutting* Alignment Error, it is not covered in this chapter. Notes displaying this problem can be found in the *Cutting Error* Chapter.

# Misaligned Faces / Backs

Misaligned Face and Back Errors have a Class Rarity rating of R2.

Misaligned Face and Back errors occur when a full sheet of currency gets out of alignment during the printing process. This alignment problem can occur when the sheet slips or jams in the mechanical guides or becomes folded so that the printed design is not properly oriented to the top or sides of the uncut sheet. When the problem is corrected for the next printing operation, the face and back will not be properly positioned with respect to each other.

The ultimate misalignment would have equal portions of two notes showing. Misaligned faces are sometimes inaccurately classified as double errors when the overprint appears to be shifted on the face. More often than not, the overprint is positioned correctly but appears to be shifted because of the face misalignment. The Overprint should be in line with the Cut (outside margins) of the note. If it is not, it is also out of alignment.

For pricing purposes, Misaligned Faces and Backs are broken down into three types: Minor, Moderate and Major.

## Large Sized Currency

Major Misaligned Face or Back Errors are unknown on Large Sized Currency.

A few examples of moderate misalignments are known to exist but are rare.

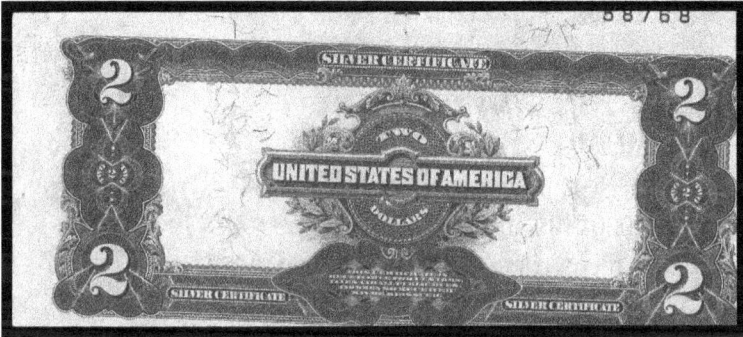

*Moderate Misaligned Back on Series 1899 $2 SC*
**F - $1,000          XF - $3,000          CU - $5,000**

*Minor  Misaligned Back on Series 1880 $5 USN*
**F - $500          XF - $750          CU - $1000**

## Misalignment of Face

A *Misaligned Face* error is a note that has a normally centered back and a face that is either shifted off center or skewed at an angle. The overprint will also be aligned properly to the cut of the note.

**Moderate Misalignment of Face**

## Misaligment of Back

A *Misaligned Back* error is a note that has a normally centered face and overprint, and a back that is either shifted off center or skewed at an angle.

**Moderate Misalignment of Face**

## Misalignment of Face and Back

A *Misaligned Face and Back* Error is a note that has a normally centered Overprint but both the face and the back are out of alignment.

**Moderate Misalignment of Face & Back**

**Additional Examples**

*Moderate Face Misaligment - $1 FRN*
*Back is Properly Aligned*
**F - $150          XF - $250          CU - $500**

*Major Face Misaligment - $1 FRN*
*Back is Properly Aligned*
**F - $500          XF - $1,500          CU - $2,500**

*Minor Face Misaligment - $2 FRN*
*Back is Properly Aligned*
**F - $50          XF - $150          CU - $250**

*Minor Face Misaligment - $10 FRN*
*Back is Properly Aligned*
**F - $25          XF - $50          CU - $100**

*Minor Face Misaligment - $20 FRN*
*Back is Properly Aligned*
**F - $25          XF - $50          CU - $100**

*Minor Face Misaligment - $100 FRN*
*Back is Properly Aligned*
**F - $125          XF - $150          CU - $200**

*Moderate Back Misaligment - $1 SC*
*Face is Properly Aligned*
F - $200          XF - $350          CU - $500

*Moderate Back Misaligment – Skewed Design - $1 SC*
*Face is Properly Aligned*
F - $300          XF - $450          CU - $600

*Major Back Misaligment - $5 FRN*
*Face is Properly Aligned*
F - $750          XF - $1,500          CU - $2,500

*Major Back Misaligment - $20 FRN*
*Face is Properly Aligned*
F - $750       XF - $1,500       CU - $2,500

*Moderate Back Misaligment – Skewed Design - $20 FRN*
*Face is Properly Aligned*
F - $300       XF - $450       CU - $600

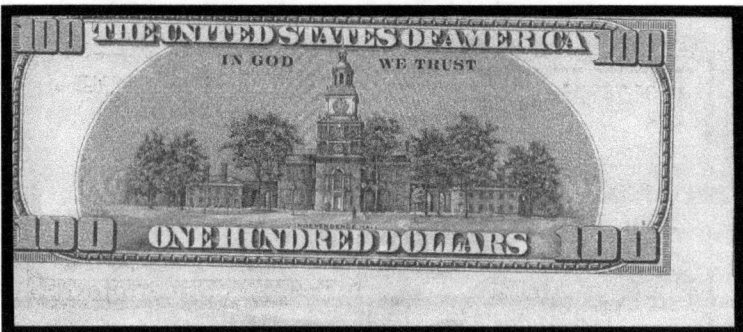

*Moderate Back Misaligment – Skewed Design - $100 FRN*
*Face is Properly Aligned*
F - $300       XF - $450       CU - $600

*Minor Face and Back Misaligment - Top of Sheet - - $1 FRN*
**F - $25            XF - $50            CU - $100**

*Minor Face and Back Misaligment - $1 FRN Web Note*
**F - $200            XF - $300            CU - $400**

*Major Face and Back Misaligment - $1 FRN*
**F - $2,000        XF - $4,500        CU - $7,000**

*Minor Face and Back Misaligment - $10 FRN Star Note*
**F - $300        XF - $450        CU - $600**

*Major Face and Back Misaligment - $20 FRN*
*Portions of 4 Notes Visible*
**F - $750        XF - $1,500        CU - $2,500**

*Minor Face and Back Misaligment - $100 FRN*
**F - $150        XF - $250        CU - $300**

## Readers Notes

# Misaligned Overprints

Misaligned Overprint Errors have a Class Rarity rating of R1.

Misaligned Overprint errors occur when a sheet of notes gets out of alignment during the overprinting process. This alignment problem can occur when the sheet slips or jams in the mechanical guides or becomes folded so that the printed design is not properly oriented to the top or sides of the sheet.

It is possible for only one of the two colors in any note that has a two-color overprint to be misaligned while the other color is correctly positioned.

## Skewed Overprint

The Overprint can also be skewed at an angle if the sheet of notes gets jammed or slips alignment during the printing process.

There are endless possibilities of skewed and misaligned overprints.

## Large Sized Currency

Major Misaligned Overprint Errors are extremely rare on Large Sized Currency.

**Reported Examples**

| Denom | Type | Series | Fr No | Serial Number | Grade |
|---|---|---|---|---|
| $1 | SC | 1899 | Fr 229 | X74921072 | F |
| $1 | LT | 1923 | Fr 40 | A36504755B | XF |
| | | | | A36504756B | VF |
| | | | | A36504759B | |
| $5 | LT | 1862 | Fr 61a | 66 | CU |

**Major Misalignment of Seal and "1"**

**Major Misalignment of Seal**

## Minor Misaligned Overprint

Some part of the face design must be impaired by the Overprint.

Very minor misalignments of the Overprint on notes that had the Series date and Signatures as part of the Overprint (See *Paper Money Creation Overview* Chapter) are considered errors if these components of the overprint impair any part of the face design. These misalignments can appear to be more dramatic than a similar shift on a note that had the Series Date and Signatures engraved on the face plate because it doesn't take much movement for the Signatures to totally obscure the titles of the officials.

**Minor Misalignment of Overprint on SC**

**Minor Misalignment of Overprint on FRN**

## Moderate Misaligned Overprint

The overprint will be misaligned by at least 3/8" in any direction.

**Moderate Misalignment of Overprint on SC**

**Moderate Misalignment of Overprint on FRN**

## Major Misaligned Overprint

The overprint will be misaligned by at least 3/4" in any direction.

**Major Misalignment of Overprint (SC)**

**Major Misalignment of Overprint (FRN)**

## Misaligned Black Portion of Overprint

The black portion of the Overprint of Federal Reserve Notes is printed after the green portion. It is possible that the sheet of notes receiving the overprint can skew or stick when advancing from the green print to the black print. When this happens, the green portion of the Overprint will be correctly positioned but the black portion will be misaligned. This misalignment is almost always low.

This error is known on every denomination of $1 through $100. It is possible to put together a denomination set with every piece having the seal in nearly the same position.

**Major Misalignment of Black Portion of Overprint**

*Minor Misalignment of Black Portion of Overprint*
F - $25          XF - $50          CU - $100

*Moderate Misalignment of Black Portion of Overprint*
F - $50          XF - $100          CU - $200

*Major Misalignment of Black Portion of Overprint*
F - $75          XF - $150          CU - $300

## Misaligned Green Portion of Overprint

A sheet that enters the overprinting press misaligned can straighten itself out during the printing process and have a properly positioned black portion of the overprint with a misaligned green portion. The methods of moving the currency through the overprinting process suggest that such an occurrence is very rare. Because of this, Misaligned Green Overprint errors are very rare.

**Moderate Misalignment of Green Portion of Overprint**

*Minor Misalignment of Green Portion of Overprint*
F - $50          XF - $150          CU - $300

*Moderate Misalignment of Green Portion of Overprint*
F - $75          XF - $200          CU - $350

*Major Misalignment of Green Portion of Overprint*
F - $100          XF - $250          CU - $500

## 1 Color in Overprint Misaligned on Silver Certificate

$1 Silver Certificates from Series 1935D through 1957B with face plate numbers between 7500 and 7999 used a multiple overprinting process that printed the Blue Overprint (Seal and Serial Numbers) and the Black Overprint (Series and Signatures) separately.

The signatures were removed from the overprinting process but not yet added to the printing plates. A 4th printing operation was used to print the signatures. This has led to some interesting overprint errors on these $1 Silver Certificates (See *Inverted Overprints* Chapter). Like the two color overprints on modern Federal Reserve Notes, one of the colors can be misaligned while the other is not.

**Moderate Misaligned Black Portion of Overprint Only**

*Minor Shift of One Color in Overprint*
**F - $200**          **XF - $400**          **CU - $800**

*Moderate Shift of One Color in Overprint*
**F - $500**          **XF - $1,000**          **CU - $2,000**

*Major Shift of One Color in Overprint*
**F - $1,000**          **XF - $1,500**          **CU - $3,000**

## Series 1996 and Later Notes

Starting with series 1996, notes of denominations $5 through $100 incorporated major changes in the overprint. One of the most significant was the relocation of the serial numbers. Prior series had the left hand serial number at the bottom and the right hand serial number at the top. The new design switched these positions. Because of this, these notes could not be overprinted on the same COPE-PAK overprinting machines as the earlier series.

A universal district seal also replaced the individual district seals of the older series. The $100 notes have this black universal seal engraved directly on the face plate. Denominations of $5 through $50 incorporate the seal in the overprint. The district is now designated by a single letter and number combination representing one of the 12 Federal Reserve Banks. This district designator is printed as part of the overprint. It is printed in black in denominations $5 through $50. It is printed in green on $100 notes.

**Interesting fact:**   The $100 notes have a one-color (green) overprint as the universal seal is printed with the face printing and there is no black in the overprint. All of the other denomination have a two-color overprint.

The term "third print" doesn't correctly describe the overprint process for these notes (Actually, it has been a misnomer for nearly as long as there have been two-color overprints.)

The following Misaligned Overprint examples show that each of the portions of the overprints on these notes is printed in a step separate (although in a single overprinting press) from the others.

Problems in these intermediate steps in the overprinting process have created some very unusual errors.

**Misaligned Universal Seal, District Designator and Treasury Seal**
**The Serial Numbers are printed in a different step**

**Misaligned Treasury Seal (Green)**
**The Treasury seal is printed in a different step**

**Misaligned Universal Seal & District Designator (Both Black)**
**The black portion of the overprint is printed in a different step**

**Additional Examples**

*Major Misalignment of Overprint - $10 NC 1902*
**F - $10,000          XF - $15,000          CU - $20,000**

*Minor Misalignment of Hawaii Overprint - $1 SC Hawaii*
**F - $500          XF - $750          CU - $1,000**

*Minor Misalignment of Overprint - $1 FRN*
**F - $10          XF - $25          CU - $50**

*Moderate Misalignment of Overprint - $1 FRN*
**F - $50          XF - $100          CU - $200**

*Major Misalignment of Overprint - $1 FRN*
*Portions of 2 Different Overprints are Visible*
**F - $700          XF - $1,500          CU - $3,000**

*Skewed Overprint – 1 Color - $1 FRN*
*Sheet was Angled During Application of Black Overprint*
**F - $600          XF - $1,200          CU - $1,500**

*Minor Misalignment of Overprint - $2 USN Star*
**F - $250          XF - $500          CU - $750**

*Moderate Misalignment of Overprint - $2 FRN*
**F - $200          XF - $400          CU - $800**

*Moderate Misalignment of Overprint - $5 FRN*
**F - $50          XF - $100          CU - $250**

*Major Misalignment of Overprint - $5 FRN*
*Portions of 2 Different Overprints are Visible*
**F - $500          XF - $1,000          CU - $2,000**

*Moderate Misalignment of Portion of Overprint - $5 FRN*
**F - $200          XF - $400          CU - $600**

*Moderate Misalignment of Overprint - $5 USN*
**F - $250          XF - $500          CU - $1,000**

*Major Misalignment of Hawaii Overprint - $10 FRN Hawaii*
F - $1,000          XF - $3,000          CU - $5,000

*Moderate Misalignment of Overprint - $10 FRN*
F - $250          XF - $500          CU - $750

*Major Misalignment of Overprint - $10 FRN*
*Portions of 2 Different Overprints are Visible*
F - $250          XF - $750          CU - $1,500

*Moderate Misalignment of Overprint – Green Seal Only - $10 FRN*
**F - $400          XF - $800          CU - $1,200**

*Major Misalignment of Overprint - $20 FRN*
**F - $150          XF - $250          CU - $400**

*Major Misalignment of Portion of Overprint - $20 FRN*
**F - $200          XF - $400          CU - $600**

*Major Misalignment of Overprint - $50 FRN*
**F - $250          XF - $750          CU - $1,500**

*Major Misalignment of Black Portion of Overprint - $100 FRN*
**F - $150          XF - $300          CU - $600**

*Moderate Misalignment of Portion of Overprint - $100 FRN*
**F - $200          XF - $400          CU - $600**

**Readers Notes**

# Overprint
# on Back

Overprint on Back errors have a Class Rarity Rating of R5.

When a sheet of notes gets turned upside down prior to it receiving its overprint, it creates the "Overprint on Back" error. The overprint must be normally positioned to the cut and rightside up in order to fall into this category.

These notes are created when a sheet of notes gets incorrectly replaced after a manual inspection for errors. It is not unusual to find a small run of consecutive notes with this error as several sheets are often removed for inspection at one time.

**The Oveprint is Printed on the Back**

## Large Sized Currency

The Overprint on Back Error is unknown on Large Sized Currency.

## Rarities Census

**Confirmed Star Notes with Overprint on Back**

| Denom | Type | Series | Serial Number |
|---|---|---|
| $5 | FRN | 1981-A | B 00056883 ★ |
| $20 | FRN | 1985 | L 02365890 ★ |

**Confirmed Natick Test[1] Notes with Overprint on Back**

| Denom | Type | Series | Serial Number |
|---|---|---|
| $1 | FRN | 1977-A | E 78779660 H |
| | | E 78879666 H |
| | | E 78879670 H |
| | | E 78899665 H |
| | | E 78979672 H |
| | | E 78979675 H |
| | | E 79059666 H |
| | | E 79059668 H |
| | | E 79139661 H |
| | | E 79219669 H |
| | | E 79219670 H |

**Confirmed Web Notes[1] with Overprint on Back**

| Denom | Type | Series | Serial Number |
|---|---|---|
| $1 | FRN | 1988-A | A 03573561 F |
| | | A 03773561 F |
| | | A 04173561 F |
| | | A 04373561 F |
| | | G 48133051 P |
| | | G 48533051 P |
| | | G 48733051 P |
| | | G 49033051 P |

[1] – See *Experimental Ink, Paper & Presses* section of the *Paper Money Creation Overview* Chapter.

**Additional Examples**

*Overprint on Back - $1 FRN*
F - $150            XF - $250          CU - $450

*Overprint on Back - $1 FRN Natick Test Note*
F - $500            XF - $1,000        CU - $1,500

*Overprint on Back - $1 FRN Web Note*
F - $1,000          XF - $2,000        CU - $4,000

*Overprint on Back - $2 FRN*
**F - $2,000          XF - $5,000          CU - $10,000**

*Overprint on Back - $5 FRN*
**F - $125          XF - $250          CU - $500**

*Overprint on Back - $10 FRN*
**F - $125          XF - $250          CU - $500**

*Overprint on Back –New Style  $10 FRN*
**F - $250            XF - $500            CU - $750**

*Overprint on Back - $20 FRN Star Note*
**F - $2,500        XF - $5,000        CU - $7,500**

*Overprint on Back - $20 FRN*
**F - $125            XF - $250            CU - $500**

*Overprint on Back – New Style $20 FRN*
**F - $250          XF - $500          CU - $750**

*Overprint on Back - $50 FRN*
**F - $250          XF - $500          CU - $1,000**

*Overprint on Back – New Style $50 FRN*
**F - $125          XF - $250          CU - $500**

*Overprint on Back – Seres 2004 $50 FRN*
**F - $500          XF - $1,000          CU - $1,500**

*Overprint on Back –$100 FRN*
**F - $500          XF - $1,000          CU - $1,500**

*Overprint on Back – New Style $100 FRN*
**F - $600          XF - $1,200          CU - $2,500**

## Readers Notes

# Inverted Overprints

Inverted Overprint Errors have a Class Rarity Rating of R5.

When a sheet of notes get turned around prior to receiving its overprint and the Overprint is placed on the face of the note upside down, it creates the "Inverted Overprint" error.

A rash of Inverted Overprints were discovered between 1976 and 1978. The BEP was under quite a bit of public scrutiny because of the more than 100 examples of this error that had made their way into newspapers, television and magazines across the country. The BEP instituted new inspection processes and guidelines but these errors continued to appear with growing frequency during that time.

To make it easier for the internal inspectors to identify these errors, the bottom margin of the currency sheets was trimmed before the face printing—a task that, prior to this change, was performed after the face printing--for Series runs after 1977A (This process was initiated in the middle of Series 1974 $50 and $100 Federal Reserve Notes).

This causes a modern Inverted Overprint on Back error note that has no other alignment problems to have normally centered (although inverted) Overprint (to the cut) but the back and face will be misaligned downward by over 3/8". Inverted Overprint on Back errors printed prior to 1977 will have normally centered backs and faces. Regardless of the Series, the back and face will be properly aligned to each other.

Depending upon its position on the sheet, a portion of the note above may also be displayed on the face and back of notes printed for Series 1977 or later. This Misalignment is very distinctive and eye catching to the inspectors.

**Note:** This error is often misclassified as a double error because two things appear to have happened incorrectly.

Inverted Overprint errors on currency with properly aligned face and backs are often referred to as Type 1. Examples on notes with the misalignment are called Type 2.

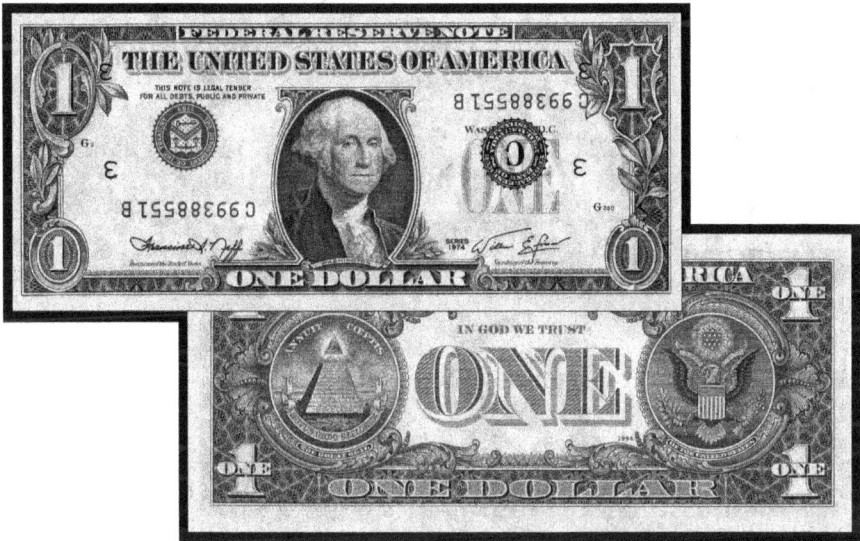

**Note Printed Prior to Series 1977A: Type 1**

**Note Printed for Series 1977A and After: Type 2**

## Large Sized Currency

The Inverted Overprint Error is extremely rare on Large Sized Currency.

**Known Examples**

| Denom. | Series | Fr No. | Serial Number | Grade |
|--------|--------|--------|---------------|-------|
| $1 / SC | 1899 | Fr 234 | D93670137A | VG |
| | 1923 | Fr 237 | K4979490B | VF/XF |
| | | | K4979491B | VF/XF |
| | | | Z45080784B | VG |
| $1 / US | 1917 | Fr 36 | D956213A | CU |
| | | | D956214A | CU |
| | | | D956215A | CU |
| | | | D956216A | CU |
| | | Fr 38 | M29859850A | AU |
| | | | M29859852A | F/VF |
| $1 / FRN | 1918 | Fr 713 | B86368354A | |
| | | Fr 719 | D11691225A | F/VF |
| | | | D11691227A | VG/F |
| | | Fr 726 | F31021151A | VF |
| | | Fr 743 | L4251193A | VG |
| | | Fr 744 | | |
| $2 / SC | 1899 | Fr 258 | AAG[1] | |
| $5 / SC | 1899 | Fr 271 | AAG[1] | |
| $5 / FRN | 1914 | Fr 851a | B46077556B | VF/EF |
| | | Fr 855a | C53195621A | VG |

[1] - AAG - Albert A. Grinnell sales of 1944 through 1947. This was the largest currency auction of its time and many rarities were cataloged without using the Serial Number in the description. Some of the notes from this sale have not yet resurfaced publicly.

## Inverted Seal

The Treasury Seal was introduced on Series 1862 Legal Tenders. Notes have been discovered with this seal upside down. The Serial Numbers on these errors are not inverted.

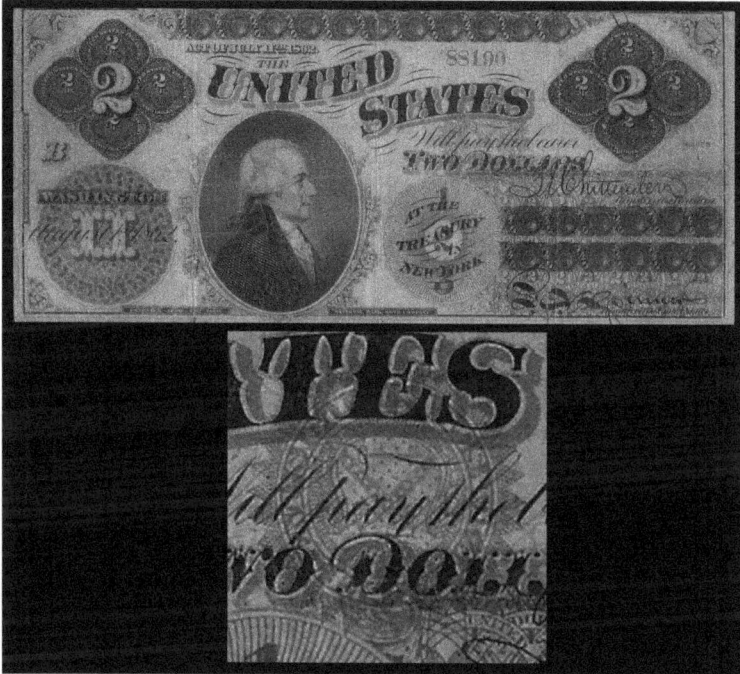

**Inverted Seal – Serial Numbers Correctly Oriented**

**Known Examples**

| Denom. | Type | Series | Serial Number |
|---|---|---|
| $2 | LT | 1862 | 88190 – Series 1 |
| | | 96165 – Series 1 |

## Large Sized Nationals

Large Sized National Currency had the signatures of the Register of the Treasury and the Treasurer engraved on the face plates but, prior to 1919, the signatures of the bank officials were added at the bank. These signatures were hand written, rubber-stamped or printed with the use of an overprinting machine. Examples are known with one or both signatures inverted.

**Inverted Signature of Cashier**

**Known Examples**

| Denom. | Type | Series | Serial Number |
|---|---|---|---|
| $5 | NC | 1902PB | 11174B[1] |
| First NB of Kansas City, MO. Charter #3456 | | | |
| $5 | NC | 1882DB | |
| German NB of Cincinnati, OH. Charter #2524 | | | |
| $5 | NC | 1882DB | 3092 | N155354[2] |
| The New Holland NB, PA. Charter #2530 | | | |
| $10 | NC | 1882 | 6645 |D550327D[3] |
| Marine NB of Milwaukee, WI. Charter #5458 | | | |
| $10 | NC | 1902PB | 5970[2] |
| The First NB of Vian, OK. Charter #10573 | | | |
| $20 | NC | 1902PB | 8496[2] |
| The First NB of Yakima, WA. Charter #3355 | | | |

[1] – Both signatures inverted and at the top of note. Sheet was placed in the overprinting machine upside down.

[2] – The Cashier's signature is inverted in its proper position. The rubber-stamp used to create this signature was upside down.

[3] – The Vice President's signature is inverted in its proper position. The rubber-stamp used to create this signature was upside down.

## Small Sized Nationals

| Denom. | Type | Series | Serial Number |
|---|---|---|---|
| $5 | NC | 1929 | A003863A[1] |
| First NB, Belleville, NY. Charter #2154 | | | |
| $5 | NC | 1929 | B001548A[2] |
| Farmers & Merchants NB. Tyrone, PA. Charter #6499 | | | |
| $5 | NC | 1929 | B013934A[1] |
| | | | D013934A[1] |
| Liberty NB & Trust Co. New York, NY. Charter #12352 | | | |
| $10 | NC | 1929 | |
| National Bank of Wrentham, MA. Charter #1085 | | | |
| $10 | NC | 1929 | D000306A[1] |
| First NB, Guttenberg, NJ. Charter #8390 | | | |

[1] – Brown portion of overprint is inverted.

[2] – Black portion of overprint is inverted.

## One Color of two Color Overprint Inverted

$1 Silver Certificates from Series 1935D through 1957B with face plate numbers between 7500 and 7999 used a multiple overprinting process that printed the Blue Overprint (Seal and Serial Numbers) and the Black Overprint (Series and Signatures) separately.

The signatures were removed from the overprinting process but not yet added to the printing plates. A 4th printing operation was used to print the signatures. This has led to some interesting overprint errors on these $1 Silver Certificates (*See Also Misaligned Overprints*).

Although modern Federal Reserve Notes also have a 2-color, 2-step overprinting process, this error is unknown on FRNs. It is also unliley, as the 2-step overprint is done in a single machine.

**Inverted Black Portion of Overprint Only**

**Inverted Blue Portion of Overprint Only**
**(Series 1935D-1957 only)**

**Additional Examples**

*Inverted Overprint - $1 SC Series 1934*
F - $3,500          XF - $6,000          CU - $7,500

*Inverted Overprint - $1 SC Series 1935D*
F - $750          XF - $1,250          CU - $2,500

*Inverted Black Portion of Overprint Only*
F - $1,000          XF - $2,000          CU - $4,000

*Inverted Overprint - $1 SC Series 1935D Star Note*
**F - $2,500          XF - $5,000          CU - $7,500**

*Inverted HAWAII Overprint  - $1 SC Hawaii*
**F - $10,000          XF - $15,000          CU - $25,000**

*Inverted Overprint - $1 FRN Web Note*
**F - $1,500          XF - $3,000          CU - $5,000**

**Inverted Overprint - $1 FRN**
F - $300            XF - $600            CU - $900

**Inverted Overprint - $2 LT Series 1953**
F - $15,000        XF - $20,000        CU - $25,000

**Inverted Overprint - $2 FRN**
F - $1,000         XF - $2,000         CU - $3,000

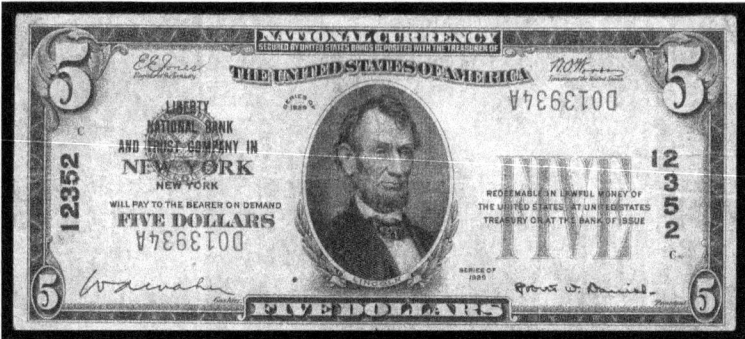

*Inverted Overprint - $5 NC*
F - $25,000          XF - $40,000          CU -

*Inverted Overprint - $5 SC*
F - $2,500          XF - $5,000          CU - $7,500

*Inverted Overprint - $5 FRN*
F - $300          XF - $600          CU - $900

*Inverted Overprint - $10 FRN – Type 1*

**F - $300            XF - $600            CU - $900**

*Inverted Overprint - $10 FRN – Type 2*

**F - $300            XF - $600            CU - $900**

*Inverted Overprint – New Style $10 FRN*

**F - $350            XF - $750            CU - $1,250**

*Inverted HAWAII Overprint - $10 FRN Hawaii*
**F - $10,000        XF - $15,000        CU - $25,000**

*Inverted Overprint - $20 FRN – Type 1*
**F - $300        XF - $600        CU - $900**

*Inverted Overprint - $20 FRN – Type 2*
**F - $300        XF - $600        CU - $900**

*Inverted Overprint – New Style $20 FRN*
**F - $500          XF - $1,000          CU - $1,500**

*Inverted Overprint - $50 FRN – Type 1*
**F - $600          XF - $900          CU - $1,200**

*Inverted Overprint – New Style $50 FRN*
**F - $750          XF - $1,500          CU - $2,500**

*Inverted Overprint - $100 FRN - Type 1*
**F - $500          XF - $750          CU - $1,500**

*Inverted Overprint – New Style $100 FRN*
**F - $750          XF - $1,500          CU - $2,500**

**Readers Notes**

# Inverted Overprint on Back

Inverted Overprint on Back Errors have a Class Rarity Rating of R9.

When a Sheet of notes gets turned upside down by flipping it top to bottom prior to the overprinting process, it will receive the overprint on the back and upside down.

A rash of Inverted Overprint errors were discovered between 1976 and 1978. The BEP was under quite a bit of public scrutiny because of the more than 100 examples of this error that had made their way into newspapers, television and magazines across the country. The BEP instituted new inspection processes and guidelines but these errors continued to appear with growing frequency during that time.

To make it easier for the internal inspectors to identify these errors, the bottom margin of the currency sheets was trimmed before the face printing—a task that, prior to this change, was performed after the face printing--for Series runs after 1977A (This process was initiated in the middle of Series 1974 $50 and $100 Federal Reserve Notes).

This causes a modern Inverted Overprint on Back error note that has no other alignment problems to have normally centered (although inverted) Overprint (to the cut) but the back and face will be misaligned downward by over 3/8". Inverted Overprint on Back errors printed prior to 1977 will have normally centered backs and faces. Regardless of the Series, the back and face will be properly aligned to each other.

Depending upon its position on the sheet, a portion of the note above may also be displayed on the face and back of notes printed for Series 1977 or later. This Misalignment is very distinctive and eye catching to the inspectors.

**Note:** This error is often misclassified as a double error because two things appear to have happened incorrectly.

## Large Sized Currency

The Inverted Overprint on Back Error is unknown on Large Sized Currency.

**Additional Examples**

*Inverted Overprint On Back – $1 FRN*
F - $1,000          XF - $2,000          CU - $3,000

*Inverted Overprint On Back – $5 FRN*
F - $1,000          XF - $2,000          CU - $3,000

*Inverted Overprint On Back – $20 FRN*
F - $1,000          XF - $2,000          CU - $3,000

*Inverted Overprint On Back – New Style $20 FRN*
F - $2,000          XF - $4,000          CU - $6,000

*Inverted Overprint On Back – $50 FRN*
F - $1,500          XF - $2,500          CU - $3,500

*Inverted Overprint On Back – New Style $100 FRN*
F - $2,500          XF - $3,500          CU - $4,500

## Readers Notes

_____

_____
_____
_____
_____
_____
_____
_____
_____
_____
_____
_____
_____
_____
_____
_____
_____
_____
_____
_____
_____
_____
_____
_____
_____
_____
_____
_____
_____
_____
_____
_____
_____
_____
_____
_____

# Inverted
# Backs

Inverted Back Errors have a Class Rarity rating of R7.

An Inverted Back error is a note that has its face and overprint positioned upside down relative to its back. This error is actually an Inverted Face note. Because a notes back is printed first, the error occurs with the face printing process.

These errors are created when a sheet of notes is fed into the face printing press rotated 180 degress from the back printing. This can happen when an entire pallet of notes from a previous run of back printing is turned around or when a single sheet is removed from the pallet for a manual inspection and replaced incorrectly. Since the sheets are flipped over before the face can be printed, this error would not be readily noticeable to the line inspectors.

To make it easier for the internal inspectors to identify these errors, the bottom margin of the currency sheets was trimmed before the face printing—a task that, prior to this change, was performed after the face printing--for Series runs after 1977A (This process was initiated in the middle of Series 1974 $50 and $100 Federal Reserve Notes).

This causes a modern Inverted Back error that has no other alignment problems to have a well center face but a back that is not only inverted but also misaligned by over 3/8". Inverted Back errors printed prior to 1977 will have normally centered backs and faces. Regardless of the Series, the back and face will be properly aligned to each other.

Depending upon its position on the sheet, a portion of the note above may also be displayed on the face and back of notes printed for Series 1977 or later. This Misalignment is very distinctive and eye catching to the inspectors.

**Note:**  This error is often misclassified as a double error because two things appear to have happened incorrectly.

Inverted Back errors on currency with properly aligned face and backs are often referred to as Type 1. Examples on notes with the back misalignment are called Type 2.

**Inverted Back Note – Type 1**

**Inverted Back Note – Type 2**

## Large Sized Currency

## Multi Denomination Sheet

Many National Bank Notes were printed in multiple denomination sheets. When a sheet of these notes gets turned around before the face printing, an unusual type of invert is created. These notes have an inverted back but it is a different denomination than the face. Although the creation of this type of error is from an inverted sheet, these errors are categorized as double denominations (See *Double Denomination* Chapter).

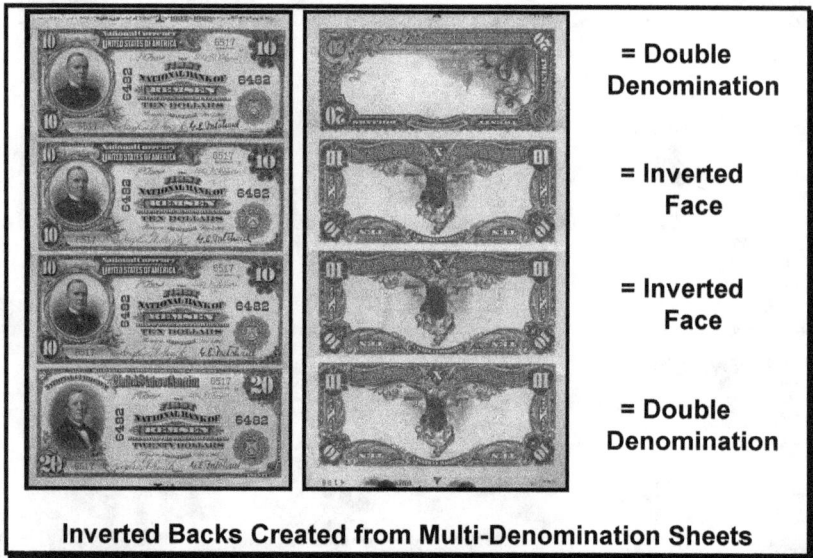

**Inverted Backs Created from Multi-Denomination Sheets**

A variety of multiple denomination sheet combinations were used on National Bank Notes creating several different combinations of Inverted Double Denomination and Inverted Back notes printed from the same sheet (*See Double Denomination Chapter*).

# Large Sized Currency

## Large Sized $1 Inverted Back Notes Census

| Denom \| Type | Series | Fr No. | Serial Number | Grade |
|---|---|---|---|---|
| $1 \| TN | 1890 | Fr 348 | Unreported | |
| | | Fr 349 | Unreported | |
| | 1891 | Fr 350 | B6939748 | VG |
| | | Fr 351 | B18966446 | F |
| | | Fr 352 | B52243743 ★ | G/VG |
| $1 \| SC | 1886 | Fr 215 | B1807759 | VG |
| | | | B6235039 | VG |
| | | Fr 216 | B16145384 | F |
| | | Fr 217 | B28469752 | VG |
| | 1899 | Fr 226 | 4426344 | F |
| | | | 59969457 | G |
| | | | 95028599 | VG |
| | | Fr 226a | A31203048 | AG |
| | | | A38606116 | G |
| | | | A52024780 | VG |
| | | | A63281013 | F |
| | | | B32486637 | F/VF |
| | | | B56649979 | F |
| | | | B82267090 | VG |
| | | | D30573339 | VG |
| | | | D38260977 | F |
| | | | D62801502 | F |
| | | Fr 227 | K2464790 | F/VF |
| | | Fr 228 | AAG[1] | CU |
| | | | M51653375 | F |
| | | | M5888780 | VF |
| | | | N24865075 | XF/AU |
| | | | N42086858 | XF |
| | | | N42086859 | |
| | | | N80198011 | VG |
| | | | N77385298 | VF |
| | | | N85856457 | VG |
| | | | N90885844 | G/VG |
| | | | R31241150 | VF/XF |
| | | | R93994950 | G/VG |
| | | | T11287101 | VG |
| | | | T46840272 | VG/F |

| Denom \| Type | Series | Fr No. | Serial Number | Grade |
|---|---|---|---|---|
| | | Fr 229 | V23234306 | G |
| | | Fr 230 | ★2211584B | CU |
| | | | Y94147184 | VF |
| | | | A41731062A | XF |
| | | | A54566826A | VG |
| | | | A90990570A | VG |
| | | | E34359998E | CU |
| | | | E24260000E | CU |
| | | | E43459997E | |
| | | | E43459998E | CU |
| | | | E43459999E | CU |
| | | | E43460000E | |
| | | | E59688025E | VG |
| | | Fr 232 | ★4183779B | G |
| | | | M35045047M | CU |
| | | | M40081891M | CU |
| | | | M51028760M | VG |
| | | | N577219N | VF |
| | | | R31181817R | VF |
| | | | R31191999R | VF |
| | | | R48575500R | VF |
| $1 \| SC | 1899 | Fr 233 | B1966486A | VG |
| | | | B29961620A | F |
| | | | B40438418A | VG |
| | | | B70961815A | F |
| | | | B72910341A | G |
| | | | B84781184A | VG |
| | | | D21642520A | VG |
| | | | R53440793R | VG |
| | | | V65051522Y | F |
| | | | V88945825V | VF |
| | | | X95238952X | F |
| | | | Y21007551Y | XF |
| | | | Y35321823Y | VG |
| | | | Y39734300Y | VG |
| | | | Y62261634Y | F |
| | | | Y65051522Y | F |
| | | | Y78764489Y | XF |
| | | | Y94228131Y | VG/F |
| | | | Z38301291Z | F/VF |
| | | | Z51540680Z | F |
| | | | Z55515328Z | VG |
| | | | Z61256642Z | VG |
| | | | Z72638796Z | F |
| | | | Z79142686Z | AU |
| | | | Z99946520Z | F/VF |

| Denom \| Type | Series | Fr No. | Serial Number | Grade |
|---|---|---|---|---|
| $1 \| SC | 1899 | Fr 234 | ★12196154B | VG/F |
| | | | D48583523A | VG |
| | | | D55126816A | VG |
| | | Fr 235 | E42748818A | VF |
| | | | E87153057A | F |
| | | | H3661234A | VF/XF |
| | | | H9012609A | XF |
| | | | H21990397A | CU |
| | | | H21990398A | CU |
| | | | H21990399A | CU |
| | | | H21990400A | XF |
| | | | H34508326A | F |
| | | | H72098069A | F |
| | | | H80784610A | XF |
| | | | K10575933A | XF |
| | | | K10575934A | XF/AU |
| | | | K10575938A | AU |
| | | | K65009881A | VG |
| | | Fr 236 | M88803743A | VG |
| | | | N2078814A | XF |
| | | | N67529849A | VG |
| | | | N78273612A | VF |
| $1 \| SC | 1923 | Fr 237 | ★1559176D | XF |
| | | | ★15182952D | VF |
| | | | A11867528B | F |
| | | | A15778547B | XF |
| | | | A67295992B | VG |
| | | | A68254999B | CU |
| | | | A70383795D | F |
| | | | B78400928D | F |
| | | | D1860830B | VG/F |
| | | | E1534016B | VG |
| | | | K23896446B | XF |
| | | | K40122887B | VG |
| | | | N2656841B | F |
| | | | N23896446B | XF |
| | | | R95851675B | VG |
| | | | V12808256B | F |
| | | | V33100720B | CU |
| | | | V33100721B | CU |
| | | | V33100722B | CU |
| | | | X4220207B | F/VF |
| | | | X68079493D | F/VF |
| | | | Z45080784B | F |

| Denom \| Type | Series | Fr No. | Serial Number | Grade |
|---|---|---|---|---|
| $1 \| SC | 1923 | Fr 238 | ★20813224D | F |
| | | | A76311869E | VG/F |
| | | | Z26441578D | F |
| $1 \| LT | 1917 | Fr 36 | A86242377A | VG |
| | | | B8657969A | VF+ |
| | | Fr 37 | K2783879A | XF |
| | | | D77019047A | CU |
| | | | E39420520A | F |
| | | | E97429498A | CU |
| | | | E97429499A | CU |
| | | | K30338956A | CU |
| | | | K75754565A | F |
| | | | AAG[1] - Cut Sheet | CU |
| | | Fr 38 | K93548416A | F/VF |
| | | Fr 39 | R23811887A | VG |
| | | | R59832902A | CU |
| | | | T55685201A | G |
| | | Fr 40 | A316229B | VF |
| | | | A4625630B | G |
| | | | A11231764B | G/VF |
| | | | A27919777B | AU |
| $1 \| FRBN | 1918 | Fr 708 | A5291161A | F |
| | | Fr 711 | B2362553A | F/VF |
| | | Fr 712 | B24636756A | VG |
| | | Fr 717 | C36303888A | VG |
| | | | C36669848A | F |
| | | Fr 718 | D11641957A | VF |
| | | Fr 720 | D29049837A | F/VF |
| | | | D37913522A | F |
| | | Fr 725 | F12463692A | |
| | | Fr 730 | H53A | CU |
| | | | H54A | CU |
| | | | H55A | CU |
| | | | H56A | CU |
| | | Fr 737 | J3903132A | |
| | | Fr 743 | L3984032A | G/VG |
| | | Fr 744 | Unreported | |

## Large Sized $2 Inverted Back Notes Census

| Denom | Type | Series | Fr No. | Serial Number | Grade |
|---|---|---|---|---|
| $2 | SC | 1886 | Fr 242 | B7455379 | G |
| | | 1899 | Fr 249 | AAG[1] | CU |
| | | | | 931650 | F |
| | | | | 5893784 | |
| | | | | 5937609 | VG |
| | | | | 13793445 | VF |
| | | | | 75738201 | VF |
| | | | | 98241554 | F/VF |
| | | | | 19986605 | VG |
| | | | | A8282329 | F/VF |
| | | | Fr 251 | D4584441 | VF |
| | | | | D4584442 | AU |
| | | | | D4584443 | CU |
| | | | | D7160040 | F |
| | | | | D12309172 | F |
| | | | | D13135951 | F |
| | | | | D19118800 | VG+ |
| | | | | D40711708 | F |
| | | | | D45669223 | CU |
| | | | | D45669224 | AU |
| | | | | D51114926 | VG |
| | | | | D52486899 | F+ |
| | | | | D57422973 | F/VF |
| | | | | D68001808 | G |
| | | | Fr 252 | E27433026 | F |
| | | | Fr 253 | E97775414 | |
| | | | | K23508297 | |
| | | | Fr 255 | AAG[1] | CU |
| | | | | M25872678 | VG |
| | | | | M25872680 | VG/F |
| | | | | M26595725 | G |
| | | | | M29980094 | VF |
| | | | Fr 256 | M88880480 | F |
| | | | | N8138687 | VF |
| | | | | N13922697 | F |
| | | | | N16963094 | G |
| | | | | N21656129 | AU |
| | | | | N23332972 | F |
| | | | | N27351805 | |
| | | | | N28394364 | F |
| | | | | N39856925 | VG |
| | | | | N52980491 | VF |

| Denom \| Type | Series | Fr No. | Serial Number | Grade |
|---|---|---|---|---|
| $2 \| SC | 1886 | Fr 258 | N73599253 | F |
| | | | N87587314 | F+ |
| | | | N90720854 | VF/XF |
| | | | N95582483 | F |
| | | | N97580387 | F |
| $2 \| LT | 1880 | Fr 50 | Z7986034 | G |
| | 1917 | Fr 57 | ★611598B | AU |
| | | | AAG[1] | CU |
| | | | A15146552A | VG |
| | | | A21925531A | EF |
| | | | A33242712A | VG |
| | | | A36987068A | VG/F |
| | | | A39823057A | VF |
| | | | A58895841A | VF |
| | | | A60916723A | VF/XF |
| | | Fr 58 | A73294431A | VG |
| | | | B9296418A | VG |
| | | | B9416162A | VF |
| | | Fr 60 | ★2828827B | VG |
| | | | ★3351684B | VG/F |
| | | | B64625224A | VG |
| | | | B96024848A | G |
| | | | D15013600A | F |
| | | | D35252501A | F |
| | | | D50712612A | F |
| | | | D67581330A | F |
| | | | D90673078A | F |
| | | | E23709134A | AU |
| $2 \| FRBN | 1918 | Fr 750 | B290135A | AU |
| | | | B290136A | CU |
| | | Fr 751 | B8063947A | Fair |
| | | Fr 760 | E158772A | F |
| | | Fr 767 | G8781579A | F |

**Large Sized $5 Inverted Back Notes Census**

| Denom \| Type | Series | Fr No. | Serial Number | Grade |
|---|---|---|---|---|
| $5 \| NC | 1902 PB | Fr 600 | 145870 | F |
| Commercial NB of Shreveport, LA. Charter #3600 | | | | |
| $5 \| NC | 1902 PB | Fr 602 | 70538 \| M713549H | F |
| NB of the Republic Chicago, Illinois. Charter 4605 | | | | |
| $5 \| SC | 1891 | Fr 267 | E7404007 | VG |
| | 1896 | Fr 270 | 33781446 | VG+ |
| | 1899 | Fr 271 | 20835679 | F/VF |
| | | | 35042468 | VG/F |
| | | | 41742049 | F |
| | | | 68960006 | |
| | | | 88071618 | AG |
| | | | 90479124 | F |
| | | | A11929748 | |
| | | | A33109985 | VG |
| | | | A43425606 | XF |
| | | | A43425608 | VG |
| | | Fr 272 | B14886806 | F/VF |
| | | Fr 273 | D40718583 | F |
| | | | D41799415 | VF |
| | | | D46388772 | VG/F |
| | | | D50094568 | VG |
| | | | D69446610 | F |
| | | Fr 274 | ★86518B | VF |
| | | Fr 275 | E63157141 | VF |
| | | | E66512537 | G |
| | | Fr 277 | M12411774 | |
| | | Fr 278 | M70584712 | AG |
| | | | M77898505 | CU |
| | | | M77898508 | XF |
| | | Fr 279 | M90637853 | F |
| | | Fr 280 | M99431036 | VF |

| Denom \| Type | Series | Fr No. | Serial Number | Grade |
|---|---|---|---|---|
| | 1880 | Fr 77 | Unreported | |
| $5 \| LT | 1907 | Fr 83 | A500986 | VF |
| | | | A6814790 | AU |
| | | | A7267896 | F |
| | | | A25598613 | VF |
| | | | A25986103 | |
| | | Fr 85 | ★358663B | VG |
| | | Fr 87 | E21708590 | VF |
| | | | E29548890 | VF |
| | | | E32326823 | F |
| | | Fr 88 | H18895944 | XF |
| | | | H22596000 | AU |
| | | Fr 91 | H99663158 | F |
| | | | K50010138 | XF |
| $5 \| FRN | 1914 | Fr 847a | A38787289A | VF |
| | | | D20173219A | G |
| | | Fr 848 | B63383638A | |
| | | | B71439434A | CU |
| | | | B71439435A | CU |
| | | Fr 849 | B85728311A | F |
| | | Fr 852 | C10681663A | XF |
| | | Fr 858 | D20173219A | G/VG |
| | | Fr 870 | G53370904A | |
| | | Fr 881 | J13544293A | XF |
| | | | J13544720A | VF |
| | | Fr 888 | L10251733A | |

**Large Sized $10 Inverted Back Notes Census**

| Denom \| Type | Series | Fr No. | Serial Number | Grade |
|---|---|---|---|---|
| $10 \| NC | 1882 VB | Fr 577 | U148693 \| 138915 | |
| Bank of Pittsburgh National Association, Pittsburgh, PA. Charter #5225 | | | | |
| $10 \| NC | 1882 VB | Fr 577 | V95408 \| 1620 | |
| First NB of Smithton, PA. Charter #5311 | | | | |
| $10 \| NC | 1882 VB | Fr 577 | | |
| Lowry NB. Atlanta, GA. Charter #5318 | | | | |
| $10 \| NC | 1882 VB | Fr 577 | V174210 \| 17022 - E | |
| | | | V174210 \| 17022 - F | CU |
| Old Citizens NB of Zanesville, OH. Charter 5760 | | | | |
| $10 \| NC | 1882 VB | Fr 577 | U109977 \| 4899 | |
| First NB of Barry, IL. Charter #5771 | | | | |
| $10 \| NC | 1882 VB | Fr 577 | V162836 \|6128 | |
| Citizens NB, Houghton, MI. Charter #5896 | | | | |
| $10 \| NC | 1882 DB | Fr 545 | R244989 | F |
| 1st NB of Northport, NY. Charter #5936 | | | | |
| $10 \| NC | 1902 DB | Fr 616 | D177259B \| 35251 | |
| Second NB. Baltimore, MD. Charter #414 | | | | |
| $10 \| NC | 1902 PB | Fr 624 | 2666 | |
| First NB, Parker Prairie, MN. Charter #6661 | | | | |
| $10 \| NC | 1902 DB | Fr 618 | E488983B \| 10317 | |
| American NB, Paris, TX. Charter #8542 | | | | |

| Denom \| Type | Series | Fr No. | Serial Number | Grade |
|---|---|---|---|---|
| $10 \| LT | 1901 | Fr 114 | 13018739 | EF |
| | | | 42546372 | VF |
| | | Fr 121 | E18814208 | F |
| | | Fr 122 | E35019808 | XF |
| $10 \| SC | 1908 | Fr 302 | A1202253 | VF |
| | | | A3921344 | F/VF |
| | | Fr 304 | D111302 | VF |
| | | | D634449 | F/VF |
| $10 \| FRN | 1914 | Fr 893b | B7670824A | AU |
| | | | B9612469A | VF |
| | | Fr 906 | A28131826A | F |
| | | Fr 907a | A41636583A | F |
| | | Fr 908 | B45246276A | CU |
| | | Fr 910 | Unreported | VF |
| | | Fr 918 | D15988788A | F |
| | | Fr 930 | G51054286A | XF/AU |
| | | Fr 944 | K5243871A | XF |
| | | | K5243872A | XF |
| | | Fr 949 | L6967581A | XF |
| $10 \| GC | 1922 | Fr 1173 | AAG[1] | VF |
| | | | AAG[1] | XF |
| | | | H62852626 | AU |

**Large Sized $20 Inverted Back Notes Census**

| Denom \| Type | Series | Fr No. | Serial Number | Grade |
|---|---|---|---|---|
| $20 \| SC | 1891 | Fr 321 | AAG[1] | F |
| | | Fr 322 | H1621823 | AU |
| | | | H1778345 | EF |
| $20 \| GC | 1906 | Fr 1185 | ★125992B | F |
| | | Fr 1186 | H15962467 | VG |
| | | | H16572299 | CU |
| | | Fr 1187 | K13702459 | |
| | | | K15433697 | VF |
| | | | K34858725 | AU |
| | | | K34858728 | EF |
| | | | K59473643 | |
| | | | K71004658 | VF |
| | | | K71058428 | VF |
| $20 \| FRN | 1914 | Fr 958 | | |
| | | Fr 978 | D15481309A | CU |
| | | Fr 988 | G10862473A | XF |
| | | Fr 989 | G16219135A | VF/XF |
| | | Fr 991a | G38632210A | VG |

**Large Sized $50 Inverted Back Notes Census**

| Denom \| Type | Series | Fr No. | Serial Number | Grade |
|---|---|---|---|---|
| $50 \| GC | 1922 | Fr 1200 | AAG[1] | VF |

**Large Sized $100 Inverted Back Notes Census**

| Denom \| Type | Series | Fr No. | Serial Number | Grade |
|---|---|---|---|---|
| $100 \| FRN | 1914 | Fr 1088 | B1726775A | XF |
| | | Fr 1098 | D496089A | VF |

[1] - AAG - Albert A. Grinnell sales of 1944 through 1947. This was the largest currency auction of its time and many rarities were cataloged without using the Serial Number in the description. Some of the notes from this sale have not yet resurfaced publicly.

**Additional Examples**

*Inverted Back - $1 SC Series 1899*
F - $750       XF - $1,500       CU - $3,000

*Inverted Back - $5 SC Series 1899*
F - $3,000       XF - $5,000       CU - $8,000

*Inverted Back - $10 LT Series 1901*
F - $3,000        XF - $5,000        CU - $8,000

*Inverted Back - $1 SC Series 1928-A*
F - $500        XF - $750        CU - $1,000

*Inverted Back - $1 SC Series 1934 Star Note*
**F - $2,000　　　XF - $3,500　　CU - $5,000**

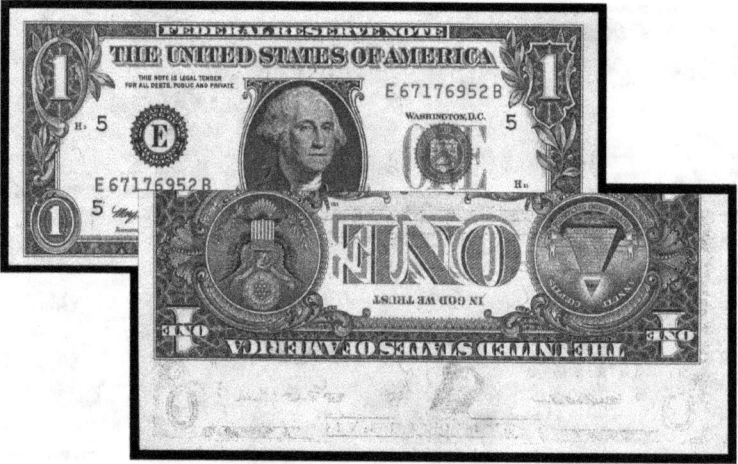

*Inverted Back from top of Sheet - $1 FRN Series 1995*
**F - $500　　　XF - $1,000　　　CU - $1,500**

*Inverted Back - $1 FRN Series 2003*
**F - $500        XF - $1,000        CU - $1,500**

*Inverted Back - $1 FRN Series 2003-A Star Note*
**F - $1,500     XF - $3,000        CU - $4,500**

*Inverted Back - $2 LT Series 1928-D*
**F - $2,000       XF - $4,000       CU - $6,000**

*Inverted Back - $5 FRBN Series 1929*
**F - $3,000       XF - $5,500       CU - $8,000**

**Inverted Back - $5 FRN Series 1985**

F - $500          XF - $1,000          CU - $1,500

**Inverted Back - $10 FRN Series 1950-A**

F - $500          XF - $1,000          CU - $1,500

***Inverted Back - $20 FRN Series 1934***
**F - $750          XF - $1,500          CU - $2,000**

***Inverted Back - $20 FRN Series 1996***
**F - $750          XF - $1,500          CU - $2,500**

*Inverted Back - $50 FRN Series 1928*
**F - $2,000      XF - $3,500      CU - $5,000**

*Inverted Back - $50 FRN Series 1974*
**F - $1,000      XF - $2,000      CU - $3,000**

*Inverted Back - $100 FRN Series 1934*
F - $3,000      XF - $5,000      CU - $7,000

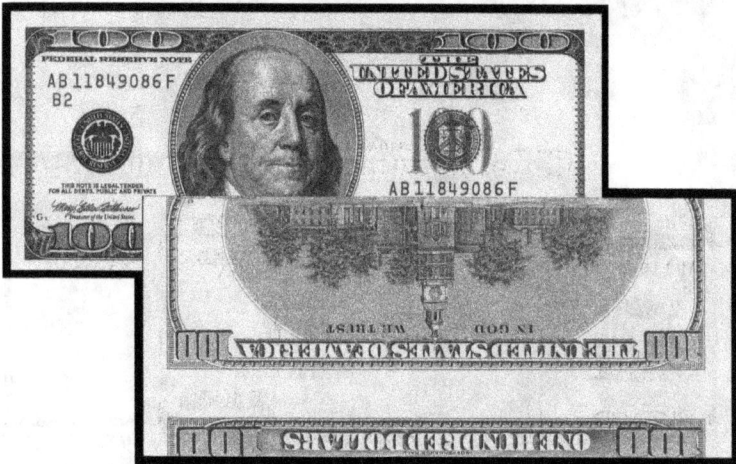

*Inverted Back - $100 FRN Series 1996*
F - $2,000      XF - $3,500      CU - $5,000

**Readers Notes**

# Cutting Errors

Full Sheets of currency go through a series of cutting operations before they become individual notes. After the face printing, 32 subject sheets are cut in half to make it easier to inspect the large sheets for errors. Immediately after the Overprints are printed on the notes, the margins of the half sheets are trimmed to a standard size and stacks of 100 are first cut into horizontal pairs (two notes, side by side) and then into individual notes.

The sheets of notes are moved through the overprinting equipment on a conveyor system that utilizes a series of mechanical fingers, guides, suction cups and jets of air. When a sheet fails to align properly during the cutting process, an unusual error note is created. A note that has the back, face and overprint all in line with each other except for the cut (outside margin will be out of alignment) is classified as a cutting error.

Notes with extra paper tabs (flags) that are the result of folds, wrinkles or tears are not covered in this chapter (See *Folds & Tears* Chapter).

# MisCut Notes

MisCut Notes have a Class Rarity Rating of R5.

A MisCut note will have the back, face and overprint all in line with each other but the cut (outside margin) will be out of alignment.

BEP inspection guidelines for modern notes state that as long as there is a white border all the way around note design, it is passable. Older notes had a more stringent inspection criteria, and if a note showed only a sliver of white margin it was considered misaligned or miscut.

**All Design Elements in line with each other**

## Large Sized Currency

There are numerous examples of minor cutting errors on Large Sized Currency, but moderate to major examples are unknown.

## National Currency

National currency was delivered to the individual banks in sheets and was cut by hand. Many Nationals display very poor cuts and are not considered errors.

## Minor
## Cutting Error

A small portion of the design of another note from the sheet or the margin selvage will be visible.

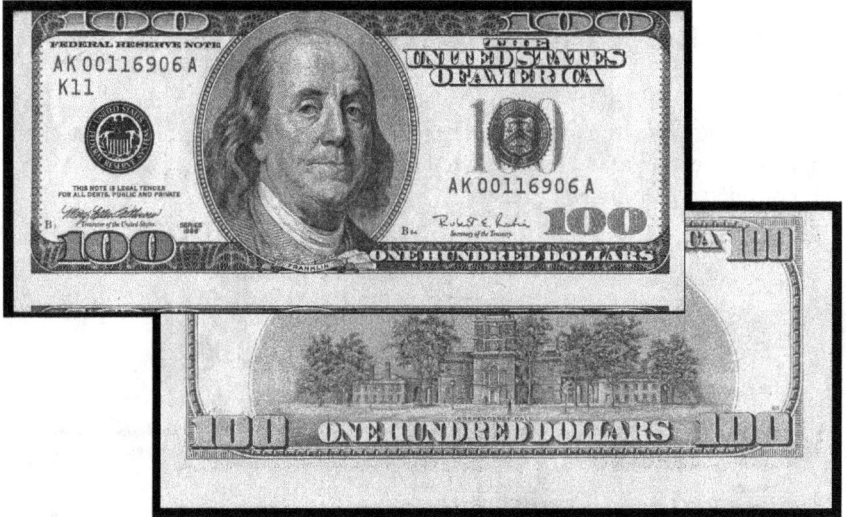

**Sliver of Note Below is Visible on the Face**

## Moderate
## Cutting Error

The cut will be misaligned by at least 3/8" in any direction.

**Portion of Note Above
Visible on the Face and Back**

# Major
# Cutting Error

The cut will be misaligned by at least 3/4" in any direction.

**Major Portion of Another Note
Visible on the Face and Back**

## Miscut Notes
## from the Same Sheet

Miscut notes from the same sheet should have the same amount of misalignment on both notes.

**Notes From Different Positions on Same Sheet**

**Additional Examples**

*Moderate Cutting Error with Skewing- $1 FRN Star Note*
**F - $200          XF - $500          CU - $750**

*Moderate Cutting Error - $5 FRN*
**F - $500          XF - $1,000          CU - $1,500**

*Minor Cutting Error - $10 FRN Star Note*
**F - $200          XF - $500          CU - $750**

*Minor Cutting Error - $20 FRN*
F - $50          XF - $100          CU - $200

*Minor Cutting Error – New Style $20 FRN*
F - $50          XF - $100          CU - $200

*Minor Cutting Error - $50 FRN*
F - $60          XF - $100          CU - $200

*Minor Cutting Error – New Style $50 FRN*
**F - $60          XF - $100          CU - $200**

*Minor Cutting Error Showing Sheet Selvage - $100 FRN*
**F - $125          XF - $175          CU - $200**

*Major Cutting Error - $100 FRN*
**F - $1,000          XF - $2,500          CU - $5,000**

## Readers Notes

# Engraving Errors

The printing plates used to print US currency are intaglio engraved. This means that the design is cut into the steel plate instead of being raised off from the plate. These plates are engraved as a mirror image of the design intended for the note. The engravers have to envision each of the elements of the design in reverse. Several of the recorded engraving errors were probably the result of this difficult task.

**Author's Note:** Several minor differences have been noticed on face plate numbers and the placement of the face plate numbers in relationship to both the check plate position and the "FW" prefix of notes printed in the Fort Worth facility. Many Series 2003 $2 notes display a face plate number that is aligned with the middle of the "FW" instead of the normal bottom alignment. I've also seen a group of $1 notes that had the plate number much closer to the face check position than normal. I've heard these differences referred to as "Proximity errors", but in truth, they aren't considered errors by the BEP. Minor variances have been documented on dozens of face plates from Series 2001, 2003 and 2003-A.

# Back Plate
# Number 1905 / 905

Some series 1974 $1 FRN's have been discovered with back plate number 905. The correct number was supposed to be 1905. Back Plate 905 wasn't used for seven years prior to the production of these notes.

All 32 subjects of the back plate were affected and it is possible to find examples from every position on the full sheet

**Known Blocks**

| Series | Block | |
|--------|-------|---|
| | A - A | G - B |
| | B - D | H - A |
| | C - B | J - ★ |
| 1974 | D - A | K - B |
| | E- C | L - B |
| | F - D | L - C |

***Back Plate 905 Engraving Error***
**F - $25**          **XF - $50**          **CU - $100**

155

# Back Plate Number 7273 / 3273

In 1981 the BEP began to sell full 32 subject sheets of Series 1981 $1 notes to the public. Shortly after these sheets went on sale, several sheets printed for the Richmond (E) District were found to have an engraving error on their backs. The back plate number for the note in Check Plate position H1 carries back plate number 7273. All other notes on the sheet have back plate number 3273. This error would never have been discovered if it weren't for the issuance of the full sheets. Once the sheets are cut into individual notes, it is impossible to tell that the notes bearing different back plate numbers came from the same sheet.

**Known Blocks**

| Series | Block |
|--------|-------|
| 1981 | E - E |
|        | E - F |

Full sheets of FRN were not available prior to 1981 so it is unknown exactly when this back plate was put into service.

Single notes from series 1977A and 1981 with back plate number 7273 would also be considered errors because the back plate numbers did not reach the 7000 mark for those series.

*Value of Full Sheet*
**CU - $350**

*Value of Single note*
**F - $25**      **XF - $50**      **CU - $100**

# Back Plate
# Number 129

3,036,480 $1 FRN's from Series 1981A and 1985 were reported to have been printed from Back Plate 129. This Plate had an engraving error on it. The Back plate number was misplaced from its standard position under the right side of the "ONE" to under the left side. All 32 subjects of the back plate were affected and it is possible to find examples from every position on the full sheet. This error was probably the result of the difficulty in envisioning the plates as mirrored images while they are engraved.

**Known Blocks**

| Series | Block | |
|---|---|---|
| | C - A | I - B |
| 1981A | H - B | L - G |
| | I - A | |
| | A - A | G - A |
| | B - A | H - A |
| | B - B | J - A |
| 1985 | D - A | K - A |
| | E – A[1] | L - A |
| | F - A | |

[1] - Several full sheets have been reported from the Richmond (E) District.

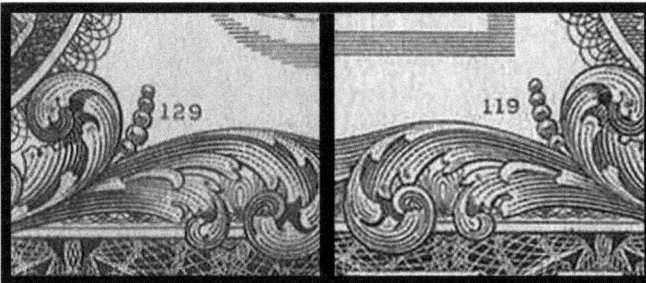

***Back Plate 129 Engraving Error***
**F - $25       XF - $50       CU - $100**

# Fort Worth
# Plate Numbering Errors

As the annual production of US currency approached 6 billion notes, it became apparent that the BEP facility in Washington DC was not large enough to accommodate the requirement for an ever increasing number of notes.

In 1991, the BEP opened its western facility in Fort Worth, Texas. Notes printed at the Fort Worth plant differ slightly from the notes printed in Washington DC. They have the FW prefix before the Lower left Check Plate number on the face of a note and a larger back plate number.

**Washington          Fort Worth**
**Face Plate Numbers**

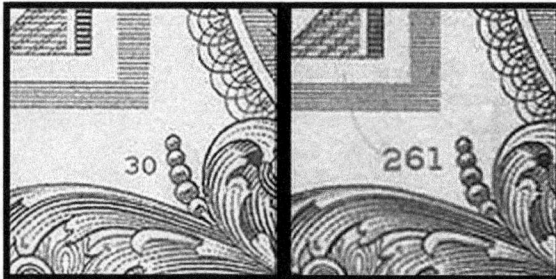

**Washington          Fort Worth**
**.6mm in Size          1.0mm in Size**
**Back Plate Numbers**

Engraving errors on both the faces and backs have been discovered on Fort Worth Notes.

**Face Plate Number 106**

Some Series 1988-A $1 notes printed in the Fort Worth facility have an engraving error on face plate 106. The plate was incorrectly engraved with larger numbers (the size of the back plate numbers notes printed in the Fort Worth facility.)

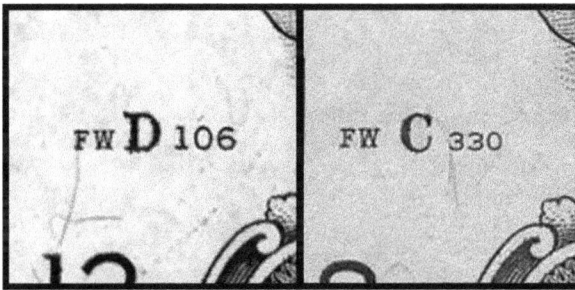

| **Face Plate 106** | | **Normal** |
|---|---|---|
| **F - $10** | **XF - $25** | **CU - $50** |

**Known Blocks**

| Face Plate 106 | |
|---|---|
| Series | Block |
| | L - ★ |
| 1988-A | L - E |
| | L - F |

## Back Plate Number 295

Some Series 1995 $1 notes printed in the Fort Worth facility have an engraving error on back plate 295. The plate was incorrectly engraved with smaller numbers (the size of those on notes printed in the Washington, DC facility.)

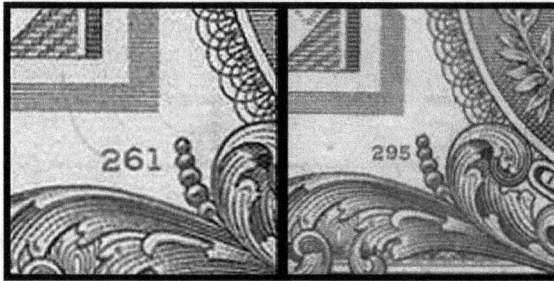

| **Normal** | | **Back Plate 295** |
| F - $10 | XF - $25 | CU - $50 |

## Known Blocks

| Back Plate 295 | |
|---|---|
| Series | Block |
| | G - ★ |
| | G - M |
| | G - N |
| | H - E |
| | I - F |
| 1995 | I - G |
| | I – H |
| | J - F |
| | K - I |
| | K - J |
| | L - W |
| | L - X |

# Missing Plate Number

All small sized U.S. currency has a plate number engraved on both the face and back plates.

A few examples are known where one of these plate numbers is missing.

**Known Examples**

| Denom \| Type | Series | Serial No. |
|---|---|---|
| $2 \| LT | 1928 | Missing Back Plate Number. Thought to be Back Plate 100. |
| $20 \| GC | 1928 | Missing Face Plate Number. Occurs in Sheet Position E. |
| $1 \| FRN | 1985 | Missing Back Plate Number. Occurs in Sheet Position E3. |

**CAUTION:** Both face and back Plate Numbers are printed in a position on a note that does not impair any part of the rest of the printed design. It is possible to remove the plate number (by abrading or erasing) without affecting any other part of the design.

*Missing Back Plate Number - $2 LT Series 1928*
**F - $500        XF - $750        CU - $1,000**

# PCBLIC
# Error

Several Series 1907 $5 Legal Tenders ("Wood Chopper" Series) notes have an engraving error on their backs.

The Obligation clause, printed on the right side of the back, states:

**THIS NOTE**
**IS A**
**LEGAL TENDER**
**AT ITS**
**FACE VALUE**
**FOR ALL DEBTS PUBLIC AND PRIVATE,**
**except Duties on Imports and Interest**
**ON THE PUBLIC DEBT.**

The "U" in the word "PUBLIC" on the sixth line is a hybrid of a "C" and a "U". By comparing it to the same word on the eighth line, it is apparent that that letter is neither and both at the same time. It appears that it was initially started to be engraved as a "U" (it has the flare at the top left of the letter associated with the "U") but was completed as a "C" (it is closed on the top loop and opened on the right side.)

This engraving error is found on all 6 sheets positions across more than a dozen back plate numbers.

*"PCBLIC" Engraving Error - $5 LT – Series 1907*
**F - $150          XF - $500          CU - $850**

# Date
# ReEngraved

Series 1875 $1 US Notes have been found to have the words "SERIES OF 1875" reengraved over top of what appears to have been erroneous initial attempt at engraving the series date.

**Known Examples**

| Denom | Type | Series | Fr No. | Serial Number |
|---|---|---|---|
| $1 | LT | 1875 | Fr 20 | H2493478 |
| | | | H2493520 |
| | 1875B | Fr 22 | B400822 |
| | 1875E | Fr 25 | H644506 |
| | | | H644508 |

All notes are printed from Face Plate 35 and from Check Plate Position "B".

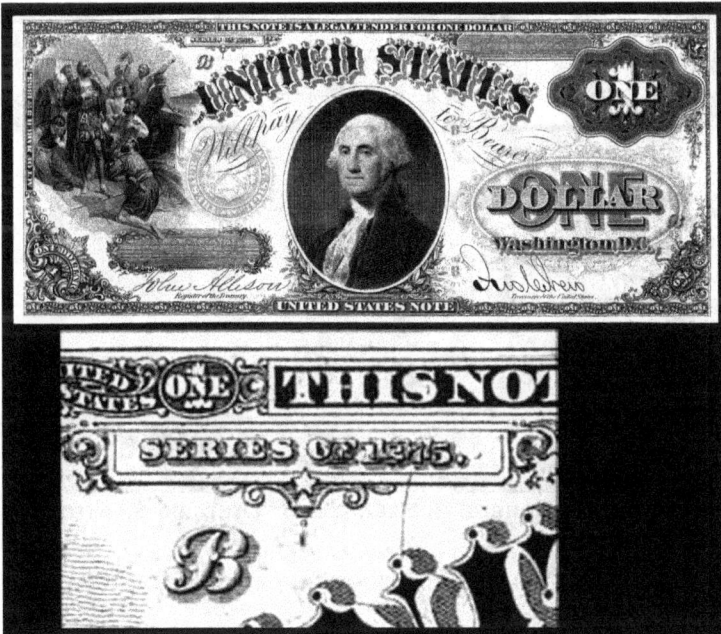

# Dropped
## "S"

A little known engraving error affected the faces of some Series 1899 $1 Silver Certificates.

The title of "TREASURER OF THE UNITED STATES." engraved on Face Plate number 2985 in Check Plate Position "B" (positions "A", "C" and "D" are believed to have been correctly engraved) had an engraving error on it. The ending "S" in "STATES" was not present. Instead, the title of "TREASURER OF THE UNITED STATE." (The ending period is present) is found on notes printed from that plate.

**Known Examples**

| Denom \| Type | Series | Fr No. | Serial Number | Grade |
|---|---|---|---|---|
| $1 \| SC | 1899 | Fr 227 | H3301878 | CU |
| | | | H13107350 | VF |

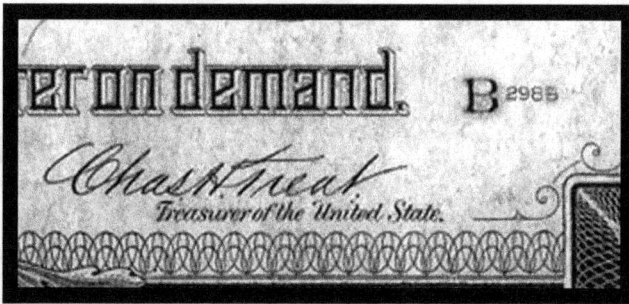

**Computer Generated Example of "Dropped S" Error**

164

# Signatures Reversed

With the exception of the $50 Legal tender notes from 1874 to 1880 (Fr 152 - 163), all other notes bearing the signatures of Treasurer and Register have the Treasurers name on the right and the Registers name on the left. The $50 Legal Tender of 1880 (Fr 164) reversed the signatures giving them the same position as the other notes.

The 1917 $1 Legal Tender (Fr 37a) note bearing the signatures of Elliot and Burke have the signature placement reversed on all notes printed from face plate 1519.

**Normally Position Signatures**

**Reversed Signatures**

| F - $300 | XF - $700 | CU - $1500 |

# Same
# Signatures

National Currency carries the engraved signatures of the Treasurer and the Register on the face of each note.

The first runs of the Series 1902 Date Back $20 National Bank Notes from The First National Bank of Oxnard, California (Charter No. 9481) have the signature of Chas. H. Treat, Treasurer of the United States engraved on their faces twice; Once in the normal position and once in place of the Registers (Vernon) signature and title.

**Computer Generated Image**
**The Signature of the Treasurer (Treat) was engraved twice**

The face plate containing this error was a multi-denominational sheet bearing 3 ten dollar notes and 1 twenty dollar note. The 3 tens did not have the engraving error.

Although the face plate with the error was used to print sheets with Serial Numbers from 1 to 3600, only a single note is known to exist. This note was sold in the Albert A. Grinnell auction and has not publicly resurfaced since that sale. Unfortunately, no Serial Number was listed in the auction catalog. A proof of the sheet that contained this error is part of the Smithsonian museum collection.

## Readers Notes

# Extra Prints

The "Extra Print" family of errors is made up of errors involving additional printings other than those intended for the note.

These additional prints can be caused by either a wet ink transfer from a freshly printed sheet of notes or piece of equipment that was mistakenly inked, from a sheet that enters the printing process multiple times or from a malfunctioning printing press.

# Offset
# Printings

Offset printings have a Class Rarity Rating of R3.

An Offset is simply a transfer of wet ink. The design meant for one section of a sheet of notes is transferred to another section or another sheet of notes. Unlike Ink Smear errors, the transferred impression will be an exact duplicate of the wet printed section of the design. In most cases, the Offset will be a mirrored image of the design it was meant for (in all cases except a Guide Roller Offset discussed later in this chapter).

An Offset error is sometimes referred to as a *Wet Ink Transfer* or a *Blanket Impression.* "Blanket" is a printer's term that refers to covering of the Impression Plate or Cylinder.

## Back and Face Offsets

During the Back and Face printing processes, full sheets of currency paper are guided between a cylinder containing 1, 2 or 4 printing plates and an equal sized impression cylinder. The Impression cylinder is a roller wrapped with cardboard and covered with a rubber coating. The printing plate cylinder and the impression cylinder are pressed together under very high pressure as a sheet of paper is passed between them.

The impression cylinder forces the paper into the inked cuts of the printing plates. Because of this, it has to be covered with a soft material in order to relieve the pressure need for the printings. If two hardened steel plates were forced together under the 25 tons per square inch of pressure needed, they would quickly crack and break apart. The soft covering of the impression cylinder allows for a slight *give* while still applying most of the pressure to the paper.

When the inked (charged) printing plate and the impression cylinder come in contact with each other without a sheet of paper between them, the ink meant for the paper is transferred to the opposite side of the next few sheets of paper to enter the cylinders. It forms a design identical to the one on the impression plate but as a mirrored image.

Prior to 1953 and the introduction of the 18 subject sheet of notes and a faster setting ink, the ink remained wet and tacky for a much longer period of time. This ink would easily transfer to another note if it came in contact with it. Strips of cardboard were manually inserted between the printed designs of each sheet to keep the sheets separated. When these strips were accidentally shifted or removed, a much darker and bolder Offset occurred.

A *Back to Face (B2F) Offset* error is a note that has all or a portion of the back of the note printed as a mirror image on the face of the note.

A *Face to Back (F2B) Offset* error is a note that has all or a portion of the face of the note printed as a mirror image on the back of the note.

A *Double Offset* error is a note that has all or a portion of the back of the note printed as a mirror image on the face of the note and the same portion of the face printed on the back of the note.

## Overprint Offsets

During the Overprinting process, half sheets of currency paper are guided between a series of printing heads and a flat impression plate. The use of the impression plate is the same as the use of the impression cylinders discussed in *Back and Face Offsets* above. When the Overprinting heads come in contact with the impression plate without a sheet of paper present, the Overprint design is transferred to the soft impression plate and is in turn transferred to the backs of the next few sheets of notes to enter the Overprinting process. The Offset Overprint onto the back of a note usually fades away after about 5 sheets pick up the ink.

An *Overprint Offset* error is a note that has the mirror image of an Overprint printed on the back of the note as a mirror image.

Guide Rollers are used to keep the paper flat and maintain its alignment and orientation. These wheels are placed so that they run in between the sections of the printed design and will not impair the wet inked design as it passes. If the Guide Roller or a sheet of currency gets out of alignment the Roller can run across the freshly printed Overprint and pick up the wet ink. This ink will be transferred to the sheets of notes that pass under it. Because this wet ink transfer occurred after the ink was on the paper, the ink will be mirrored on the roller but will transfer to the sheets correctly printed.

A *Guide Roller Offset* error is a note that has a portion of another Overprint transferred to its face from a misaligned guide roller. This is the only type of offset that is not a mirrored image.

## Partial Offsets

A Partial Offset of either the face or the back is created when a small portion of the printing cylinder comes in contact with the impression cylinder. This often happens when the sheet is torn or folded.

A partial Offset of the Overprint is created when only a portion of the Overprint printing head comes in contact with the impression plate below. This often happens when the sheet is torn or folded. This can also happen when the previous sheet does not advance enough to exit the Overprinting equipment.

## Multiple Offsets

Because an Offset print will be transferred to multiple notes, it is possible to have a note with two separate Partial Offset printings on the same side. One could be moderately dark (a third impression from the first paper fold) and a separate could be Very Dark (a first impression from a fold in another sheet of paper).

## Variance in Darkness

The ink on the impression cylinder or plate usually fades after (about) 5 sheets receive the Offset. Each Offset gets lighter until the ink is finally wiped clean or dries. For pricing purposes, Offsets are broken down into two types: Light and Dark. The first two Offset impressions are usually considered dark. There is very little price differences within the lighter notes.

**3 Note Set Displaying the Gradual Lightening of the Offset**

## Face to Back

A *Face to Back (F2B) Offset* error is a note that has all or a portion of the face of the note printed as a mirror image on the back of the note.

The Face to Back Offset is the most common type of Offset because ink is transferred to the back of the note during the face printing process and after the most stringent back inspection. Although the back is inspected again (often several more times), more of these errors escape detection because of this.

**Partial Face to Back (F2B) Offset**

**Complete Face to Back (F2B)Offset**

## Back to Face

A *Back to Face (B2F) Offset* error is a note that has all or a portion of the back of the note printed as a mirror image on the face of the note. This Offset occurs before the face printing operation.

**Partial Back to Face (B2F) Offset**

**Complete Back to Face (B2F) Offset**

## Double Offset

Very rarely, a note will be found that has a portion of the back offset onto the front and a portion of the front offset to the back in the exact same position and the same darkness. If a sheet is torn or folded during the back printing, some of the subsequent sheets will pick up the offset in the shape of the fold or the tear.

The folded or torn sheet will end up below the Offset sheets in the pallet. After drying, the pallet of sheets is flipped over for the face printing. This process will again put the folded or torn sheet before the sheets with the Offset and the subsequent sheets (the same sheets that picked up the back offset) will get the Face Offset as well. As long as the problem with the original sheet remains unchanged, the two Offsets will be identical shaped and in the same positions on both sides of the note.

There are no known examples of Double Offsets where the Offset impressions are 100% complete.

**The Face and Back Display an Identical Partial Offset**

## Overprint

An *Overprint Offset* error is a note that has the mirror image of an Overprint printed on the back of the note as a mirror image.

The most desired note (the darkest Offset) has offset of one serial number away from the normal one on the face. Several notes will pick up the Offset and the serial numbers on the back will get farther apart and lighter.

**Complete Overprint Offset**

## Offset of 1 Color of 2 Color Overprint

It is possible for a sheet of notes to advance improperly while in the Overprinting presses and to miss 1 color of the 2 color Overprint. If the missing Color is applied to the impression plate, several subsequent sheets will pick up the one color Offset impression on their backs.

**Offset of 1 Color of 2 Color Overprint**

## Guide Roller Offset

A *Guide Roller Offset* error is a note that has all or a portion of another Overprint transferred to its face from a misaligned guide roller. This is the only type of offset that is not a mirrored image (See *Overprint Errors* earlier in this chapter).

**Guide Roller Offest of Serial Number (Rotated 90°) and Seal**
**Computer Enhanced to Display Error.**
**Guide Roller Offsets are Never Dark.**

## Torn Notes

When a sheet of notes is torn prior to any one of the printing operations, the Offset impressions on subsequent sheets will match the size and shape of the tear. Some interesting looking errors have been created when a hole is torn in the sheet.

**Irregular Partial Offset Matches the Shape of the Tear**

## Large Sized Currency

While several examples of partial Offsets are available, complete Offsets are unknown on Large Sized Currency.

**Partial F2B Offset Along Right Side - Series 1899 $1 Silver Cert.**

**Complete Offset Of Signatures - Series 1862 $5 Legal Tender**

**Additional Examples**

*Partial F2B Offset – Dark - $1 FRN*
**F - $15            XF - $30            CU - $50**

*Full B2F Offset - $1 SC*
**F - $100            XF - $200            CU - $300**

*Full B2F Offset - $1 FRN*
**F - $75            XF - $150            CU - $250**

*Full F2B Offset - $1 FRN*
F - $75            XF - $150            CU - $200

*Complete Offset of Overprint - $1 SC*
F - $500            XF - $1,000            CU - $1,500

*Complete Offset of Overprint - $1 FRN*
F - $100            XF - $250            CU - $400

*Guide Roller Offset of Serial Numbers - $1 FRN*
F - $200          XF - $350          CU - $500

*Guide Roller Offset of Seal and District Number - $2 FRN*
F - $100          XF - $200          CU - $300

***Full B2F Offset- Dark - $2 FRN***
**F - $500          XF - $1,000          CU - $1,500**

***Nearly Full F2B Offset - $2 FRN***
**F - $500          XF - $1,000          CU - $1,500**

***Partial B2F Offset – Dark - $5 FRN***
**F - $15          XF - $30          CU - $50**

*Full B2F Offset- Dark - $5 FRN*

**F - $75          XF - $150          CU - $250**

*Full F2B Offset- Dark - $5 FRN*

**F - $75          XF - $150          CU - $250**

*Full B2F Offset - $10 FRN*

**F - $75          XF - $150          CU - $250**

*Full F2B Offset - $10 FRN*
F - $75          XF - $150          CU - $200

*Partial Offset of Overprint - $10 FRN*
F - $50          XF - $100          CU - $200

*Full B2F Offset - $20 FRN Star Note*
F - $500          XF - $1,000          CU - $1,500

*Full B2F Offset – Dark - $20 FRN*

F - $75            XF - $150            CU - $250

*Full F2B Offset – Dark - $20 FRN*

F - $75            XF - $150            CU - $250

*Partial B2F Offset - $20 FRN*

F - $15            XF - $30            CU - $50

*Partial Double Offset – Same Pattern on Both Sides - $20 FRN*
**F - $100          XF - $200          CU - $300**

*Full B2F Offset – Dark - $50 FRN*
**F - $150          XF - $400          CU - $750**

*Full B2F Offset – $100 FRN*

**F - $250            XF - $500            CU - $750**

*Full F2B Offset – $100 FRN*

**F - $200            XF - $400            CU - $650**

*Full B2F Offset – $100 FRN*

**F - $250            XF - $500            CU - $750**

## Readers Notes

# Multiple Impressions

Multiple Impressions have a Class Rarity Rating of R9.

A Multiple Impression error is a note with an extra printing of the back, face or Overprint. This extra printing can be either a portion of the design or the entire printing.

Multiple Impressions are often called Double Impressions because two distinct impressions of the design are visible. There are a few isolated instances where three or more printings are visible, and the term Multiple Impression encompasses these errors as well.

Multiple Impressions fall into two categories: Standard and Non-Standard.

The Standard Multiple Impression has the extra printing almost on top of the original design. It looks as if it went through the printing process at least twice.

The Non-Standard Multiple Impression has the extra printing at an angle, inverted in relationship to the original design, on the wrong side of the note or of a different denomination. These errors are very eye appealing and tell a story of something wrong that is far more drastic than a sheet of notes running through a printing press twice.

## Large Sized Currency

Multiple Impressions are unknown extremely rare on Large Sized Currency.

**Another Complete Serial Number is Found on This Note**

## Large Sized Nationals

Large Sized National Currency had the signatures of the Register of the Treasury and the Treasurer engraved on the face plates, but, prior to 1919, the signatures of the bank officials were added at the bank. These signatures were hand written, rubber-stamped or printed with the use of an overprinting machine. Examples are known with these signatures doubled.

**Signatures Double Printed**

## Standard Multiple Impressions

The Standard Multiple Impression has the extra printing almost on top of the original design. It looks as if it went through the printing process at least twice.

**Face of Note Was Printed Twice.**

## Plate Numbers on Multiple Impressions

The BEP's rotary presses are equipped with different types of printing cylinders that can accommodate 1, 2 or 4 printing plates. Consecutive notes printed the single plate press will have plate numbers that are all the same. Notes printed on the 2 plate press will have plate numbers that duplicate every other note and notes printed on the 4 plate press will have duplicate plate numbers every 5th note. This printing anomaly has created some Multiple Impression errors that display the same plate numbers and some errors that display different plate numbers.

## Partial Doubling

Partial Doubling occurs when a previously printed sheet of currency reenters the printing press on top of another sheet. If these sheets are not aligned exactly on top of each other, the printed sheet can obtain a portion of the designs meant for the other sheet. This partial doubling stops abruptly in a straight line (the edge of the other sheet.)

**Partial Double Impression of Face**

## Loose Cylinder

A Loose Cylinder Multiple Impression error occurs when the pressure between the printing plate cylinder and the impression cylinder is not kept constant or when one of the cylinders is loose. When the pressure changes or the cylinder moves, the sheet of notes that is being printed is allowed to move slightly. This movement can cause the section that is in contact with the printing plate to be double printed.

**Doubling of Black Overprint**
**Caused by a Loose Impression Cylinder**

## Multiple Impressions of Overprint

Multiple Impressions of the Overprint errors have two distinct (full or partial) Overprints on the face of the note. The note appears to have been run through the Overprinting machine multiple times. If the Serial Numbers are printed multiple times, the numbers will be different.

The vast majority of Multiple Impressions of Overprints have only a partial Impression of the extra print.

**Partial Double Impression of Overprint**

**Double Impression of Complete Overprint on $2 FRN**

## Overprinting Machine Bounce

Multiple printings of one color of a two-color Overprint can be created when the electronic detectors in the COPE-PAK machines stop the Overprint machine when an error is detected. The pneumatic (pressure controlled with air) print heads can "bounce" on the sheet several times (as the air pressure is slowly released from them) leaving a very dark seal or distinct multiple impressions (if the sheet continues to move slightly) of one of the colors in the Overprint. Machine Bounce errors that have multiple printings of the Serial Number will always display the same Serial Number.

**Machine Bounce Multiple Print Error**
**Three Green Overprints with Same Serial Number**

## Non-Standard Multiple Impressions

The Non-Standard Multiple Impression has the extra printing at an angle, inverted in relationship to the original design, on the wrong side of the note or of a different denomination.

**Multiple Impression of Face on Back**
**Skewed at Dramatic Angle**

## Complete Multiple Impression of Back on Face

The rarest Non-Standard Multiple Impression is a note that has a correctly positioned back printed over its face. The extra back printing is equally as dark as the normal back printing and the back plate numbers are the same on all known examples of this error.

**Non-Standard Multiple Impression.**
**Complete Back Design Printed on the Face.**

**Additional Examples**

**Standard Multiple Impressions**

*Multiple Impression of Face Print*
**F - $750          XF - $1,500          CU - $3,000**

*Multiple Impression of Overprint - $1 FRN*
**F - $5,000        XF - $10,000      CU - $15,000**

*Complete Double Impression of Overprint - $2 FRN*
**F - $7,500        XF - $15,000       CU - $22,000**

**Complete Double Impression of Face - $5 FRN**
F - $750              XF - $1,500          CU - $3,000

**Double Impression of Overprint - $5 FRN**
**First Impression is Weak**
F - $5,000           XF - $10,000        CU - $15,000

**Complete Double Impression of Back - $5 FRN**
**F - $750          XF - $1,500          CU - $2,500**

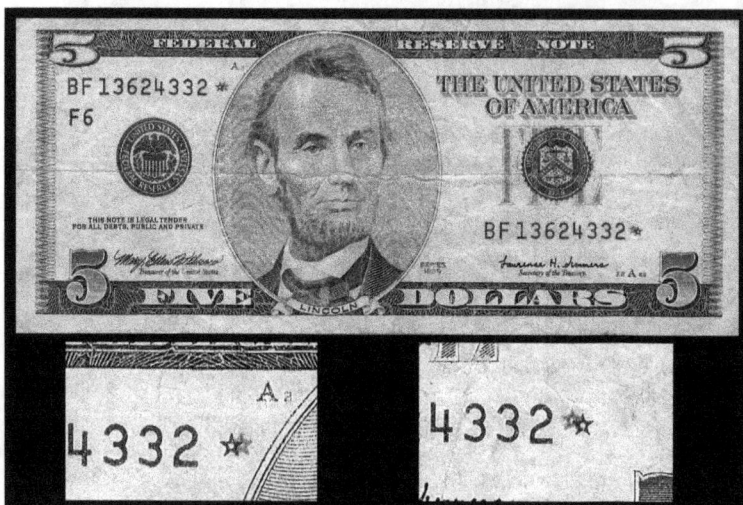

**Loose Numbering Block - $5 FRN Star Note**
**F - $500          XF - $1,000          CU - $2,000**

*Complete Double Impression of Face - $10 FRN*
**F - $750          XF - $1,500          CU - $3,000**

*Loose Impression Cylinder Doublingof Back - $10 FRN*
*Examples are known with 2, 3 and 4 Impressions*
**F - $250          XF - $500          CU - $750**

*Complete Double Impression of Back - $20 FRN*
F - $750          XF - $1,500          CU - $2,500

*Complete Double Impression of Overprint - $20 FRN*
F - $7,500          XF - $15,000          CU - $22,000

*Double Impression of Series Date - $20 FRN*
**F - $250          XF - $500          CU - $1,000**

*Loose Impression Cylinder Affecting Black Portion of Overprint*
**F - $75          XF - $150          CU - $200**

*Partial Double Impression of Face – Top of Note - $100 FRN*
**F - $250            XF - $500            CU - $1,000**

*Complete Double Impression of Back - $100 FRN*
**F - $750            XF - $1,500            CU - $2,500**

**Additional Examples**

**Non-Standard Multiple Impressions**

*Back is Design is Printed Inverted on the Face - $1 FRN*
**F - $2,000      XF - $3,000      CU - $4,000**

***Multiple Face Designs Printed At Angle On Back - $1 FRN***
**F - $2,000          XF - $3,000          CU - $4,000**

***Multiple Back Designs Printed At Angle On Face - $1 FRN***
**F - $2,000       XF - $3,000       CU - $4,000**

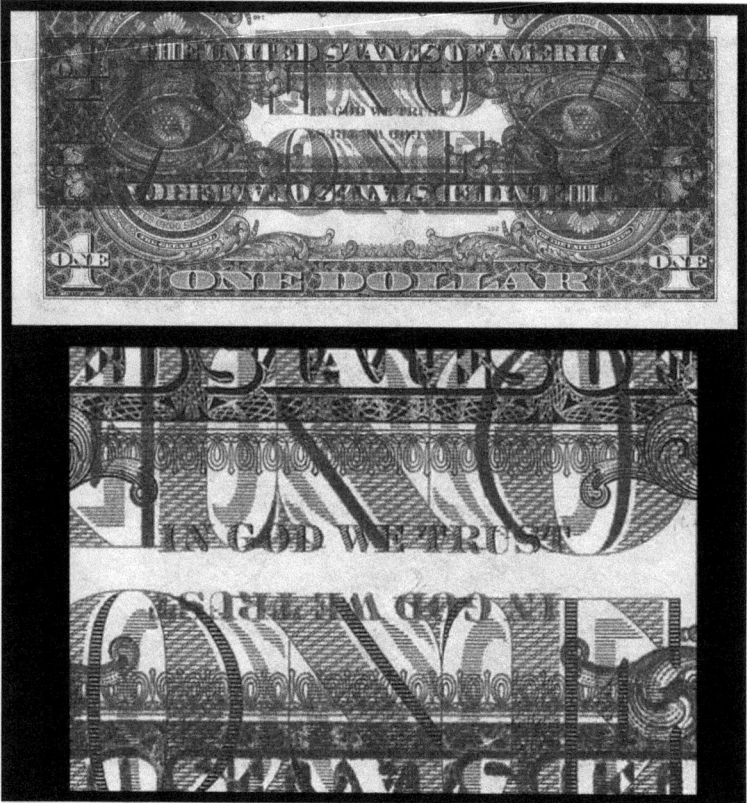

*Second Back Printing Inverted - $1 FRN*
**F - $1,000          XF - $2,000          CU - $3,000**

**Back Design Printed At Angle On Face - $5 FRN**
F - $2,000          XF - $3,000          CU - $4,000

*Second Back Printing Inverted - $5FRN*
**F - $1,000        XF - $2,000        CU - $3,000**

***Back Design Inverted and At Angle on Face - $20 FRN***
**F - $2,000          XF - $3,000          CU - $4,000**

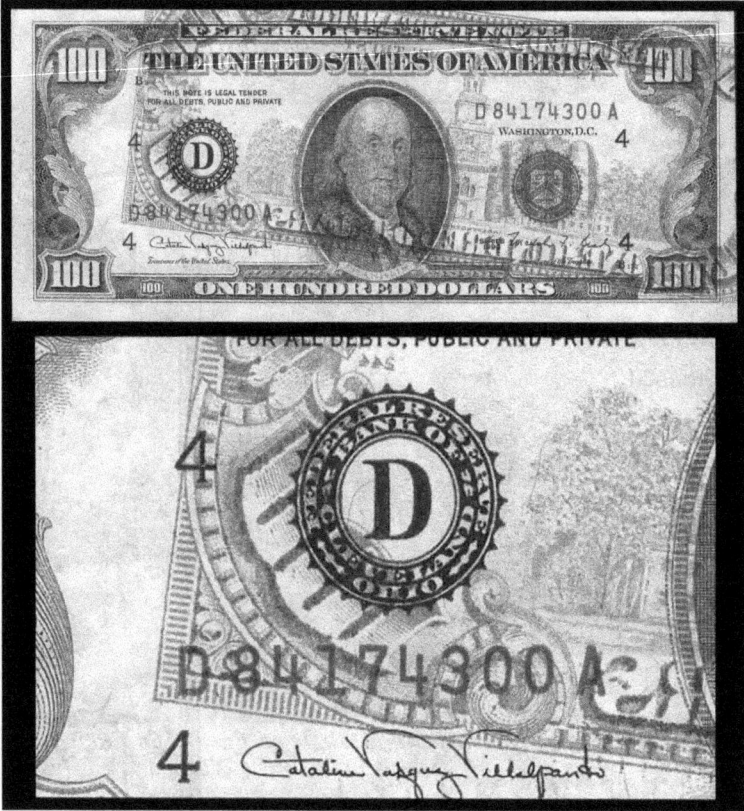

*Back Design Printed at Angle on Face - $100 FRN*
*Image is Mirror Like an Offset, but Skewed*
**F - $2,000          XF - $3,000          CU - $4,000**

# Readers Notes

# Folds and Tears

During each of the printing process, the sheets are moved and aligned with the help of conveyor systems, mechanical fingers and guides, suction cups and jets of air.

The sheets are fed into the printing cylinders from bottom to top. Once they exit that printing operation, they can be moved laterally to other conveyors with the help of guide wheels that can catch the edges and corners of the sheets as they speed down the conveying system.

These guides are thought to be the largest contributors to corner folds and tears that often result in printing errors.

Many mechanisms, rollers and sheet guides are also present that could cause paper to catch and be folded over. Some of the sheet guides are present to ensure that this does not happen and these guides will often unfold a sheet that has been folded. Many notes with folds that have affected the printing are eventually cut correctly after having been unfolded by these mechanisms.

Prior to the introduction series 1957 Silver Certificates, the method of Intaglio printing required the paper to be wet in order to make it soft enough to be forced into the cuts of the printing plates to pick up the ink and hold it onto the paper while it dried. The paper was delivered from the manufacturer already dampened (*mill wet*). The wet paper was easily wrinkled.

Some interesting errors occur when a sheet gets folded before a printing operation but unfolded prior to the cutting operation.

# Gutter Folds

Gutter Folds have a Class Rarity Rating of R1.

A Gutter Fold is a fold in the paper that leaves a blank unprinted streak on the note when the fold is opened. If the fold affects the back or face printing, the unprinted streak will be a white gutter through the design. Folds affecting only the Overprint will not have the "tell tale" white gutter but will split the affected portions of the Overprint.

Gutter Folds are one of the most common types of Error to escape the BEP and be found in circulation. Often, these errors appear normal until the fold or wrinkle is opened. It is not uncommon to see Gutter Folds on circulated notes where the gutter is bright white while the rest of the note is dirty and worn. This happens when the fold remains closed for quite some time during the circulation of the note. When the fold finally does open, the hidden paper under the fold is bright and fresh looking.

Gutter Folds can occur during the printing process or during the paper creation process. The folds that are created during the paper creation process are usually valleys or pockets in the paper where the paper has been stretched. The paper all around the valley will appear normal and the fold will not be able to be straightened out by pulling on the surrounding paper.

If the paper remains folded through the cutting process, the design on both sides of the fold may appear to be out of alignment.

## Large Sized Currency

Gutter Folds are the most common type of errors found on Large Sized currency. Numerous examples exist with Gutter Folds affecting one side, both sides and containing multiple folds.

**Single Gutter Fold - $1 LT Series 1917**

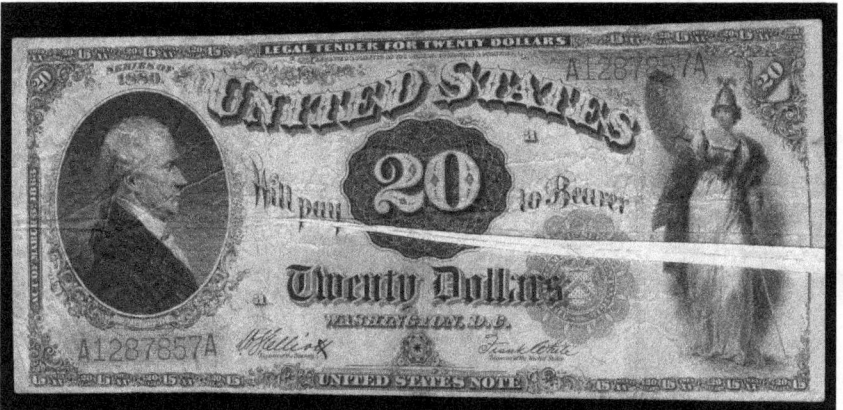

**Massive Gutter Fold - $20 LT Series 1880**

**Additional Examples**

*Large Gutter Fold  - $1 SC*
F - $150            XF - $300            CU - $450

*Massive Gutter Fold - $1 FRN*
F - $100            XF - $250            CU - $500

*Gutter Fold - $2 FRN*
F - $100            XF - $200            CU - $400

*Butterfly Fold - $5 FRN*

F - $500          XF - $1,000          CU - $1,500

*Gutter Fold - $10 FRN*

F - $500          XF - $1,000          CU - $1,500

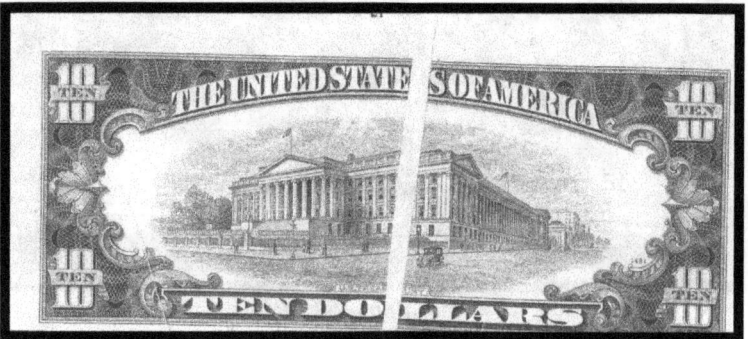

*Gutter Fold  - $10 FRN*

F - $125          XF - $150          CU - $200

**Gutter Fold - $20 FRN**

F - $150            XF - $300            CU - $450

**Multiple Gutter Folds - $50 FRN Star Note**

F - $200            XF - $300            CU - $400

**Gutter Fold - $100 FRN**

F - $125            XF - $150            CU - $200

*Multiple Gutter Folds - $100 FRN*
**F - $500            XF - $750            CU - $1,000**

*Gutter Fold - $500 FRN*
**F - $2,000          XF - $3,000          CU - $4,000**

*Gutter Fold - $1,000 FRN*
**F - $3,000          XF - $6,000          CU - $9,000**

## Readers Notes

_____

_____

_____

_____

_____

_____

_____

_____

_____

_____

_____

_____

_____

_____

_____

_____

_____

_____

_____

_____

_____

_____

_____

_____

_____

_____

_____

_____

_____

_____

_____

_____

_____

_____

_____

_____

_____

_____

_____

# Unprinted Folds

Unprinted Fold Errors have a Class Rarity Rating of R6.

An Unprinted Fold error is a note that has extra paper attached to it from the original sheet of notes. This extra paper will be the result of a foldover or a tear that remained intact during the cutting process.

The Extra Paper (flag) will often display a portion of an adjoining note on the sheet or portions of things that are printed in the margins. These things are called sheet selvage and include printing plate numbers, alignment guides, alignment holes and the initials of the people who engraved portions of the printing plates.

## Large Sized Currency

Several examples of Unprinted Fold Errors on Large Sized Currency are known to exist but all are very rare.

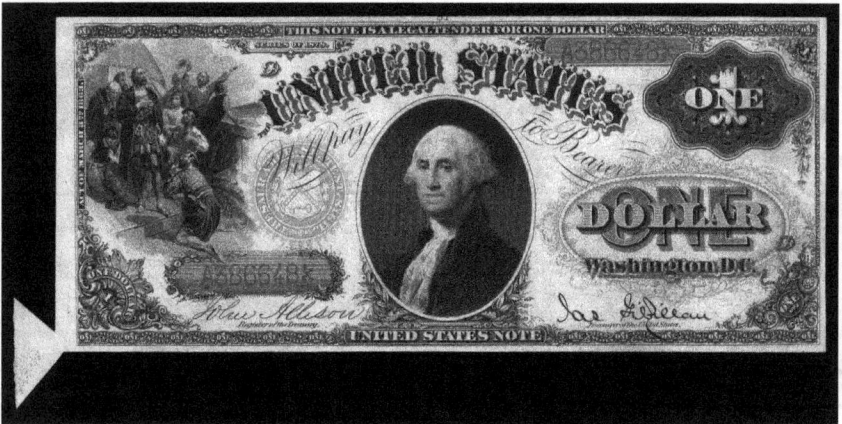

*Unprinted Butterfly Fold - $1 LT Series 1878*

## Unprinted Folds

These errors can take on two different appearances. When the fold or tear is properly closed, the note will usually be the same size and shape as a regular note (or may have a section appear to be missing due to the fold or tear) and are often found in new packs of 100 notes. When the fold or tears is opened, the note has an extra flag of paper attached to it.

The folds always remain folded and the tears remain closed through the cutting process or the affected portion would be cut away and the note would appear normal or have a portion missing.

**Fold Not Affecting Print – Closed**

**Fold Not Affecting Print - Opened**

**Additional Examples**

*Unprinted Fold - $1 SC*
F - $75              XF - $200              CU - $300

*Moderate Unprinted Fold - $1 FRN*
F - $100             XF - $250             CU - $400

*Massive Unprinted Fold - $1 FRN*
*Portions of 2 Additional Notes are Visible*
F -                 XF - $3,000           CU - $4,000

*Massive Unprinted Fold – $1 FRN*
*3/4 of the Note Below Visible*
**F -**             **XF - $4,000**       **CU - $7,500**

*Moderate Unprinted Fold - $2 FRN*
**F - $200**         **XF - $350**       **CU - $500**

*Unprinted Double Fold - $5 FRN*
**F - $200          XF - $350          CU - $500**

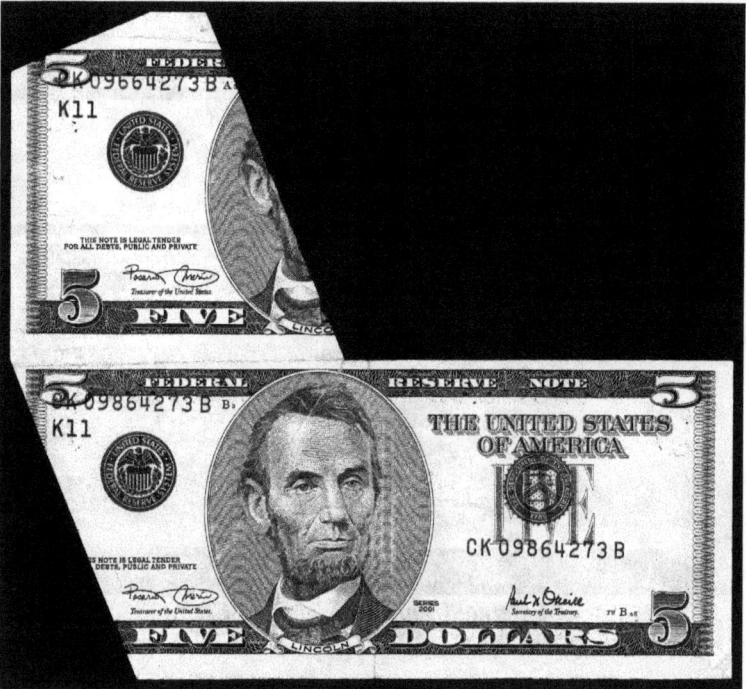

*Massive Unprinted Fold - $5 FRN*
*When Closed, the Foldover Completely Covers the Face*
**F -                XF - $3,000          CU - $4,000**

*Moderate Double Unprinted Fold - $10 FRN*
**F - $200        XF - $350        CU - $500**

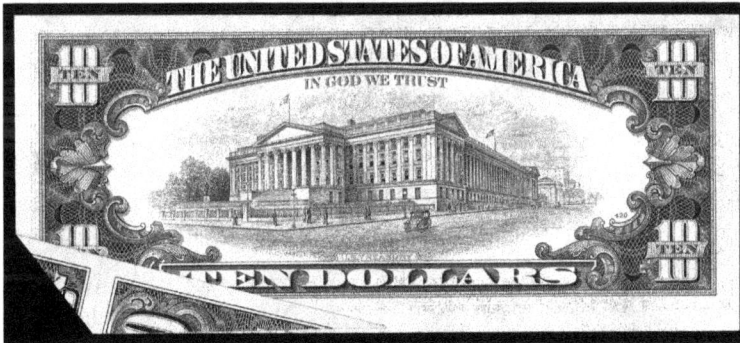

*Unprinted Fold Toward Back - $10 FRN*
**F - $200        XF - $350        CU - $500**

*Unprinted Fold - $20 FRN*
**F - $25        XF - $50        CU - $75**

*Moderate Unprinted Fold - $50 FRN*

F - $200          XF - $350          CU - $500

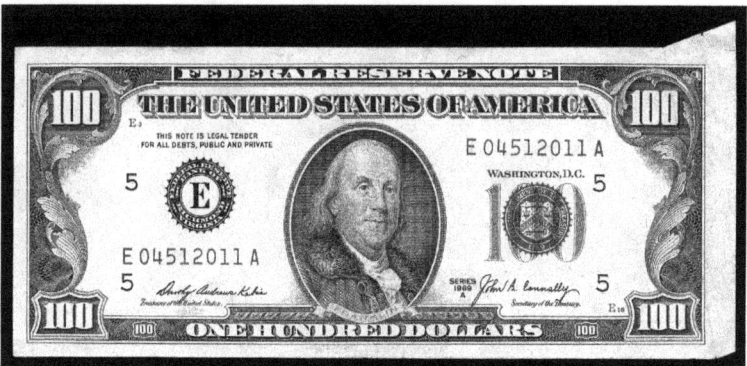

*Minor Unprinted Fold - $100 FRN*

F - $125          XF - $150          CU - $200

*Major Double Unprinted Fold - $100 FRN*

F -                    XF - $4,000        CU - $6,000

**Readers Notes**

# Printed
# Folds & Tears

Printed Fold Errors have a Class Rarity Rating of R8.

A *Printed Fold* error is a note that has a portion of its design impaired or obstructed by a portion of the sheet the note was printed on. The obstructed print may be displayed on another portion of the note, on an extra flag of paper attached to the note, or be missing altogether. The obstruction can be a foldover where no print is on fold. If a note if folded backwards prior to the overprinting, a portion of the overprint will be missing (due to the fold) but will not be on the note.

The Extra Paper (flag) will often display a portion of an adjoining note on the sheet or portions of sheet selvage (printing plate numbers, alignment guides, alignment holes, etc.).

On modern currency, most minor Foldovers are diagonal at a corner and affect notes from the A1, D2, E1, H2, A3, D4, E3, and H4 sheet positions (corners of half sheets).

| A1 | E1 |  | A3 | E3 |
|----|----|--|----|----|
| B1 | F1 |  | B3 | F3 |
| C1 | G1 |  | C3 | G3 |
| D1 | H1 |  | D3 | H3 |
| A2 | E2 |  | A4 | E4 |
| B2 | F2 |  | B4 | F4 |
| C2 | G2 |  | C4 | G4 |
| D2 | H2 |  | D4 | H4 |

## Large Sized Currency

The Folds and Tears Affecting Prints Error is extremely rare on Large Sized Currency.

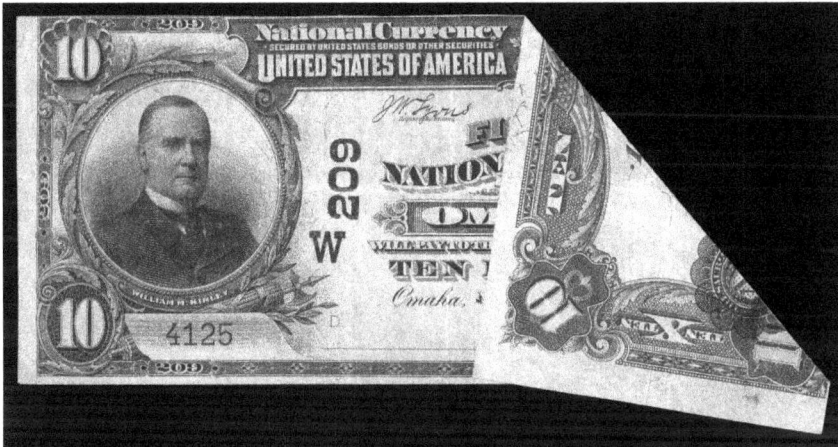

**Printed Fold - $10 National Currency Series 1902**
**Portion of Oveprinted is Printed on the Back.**

**Printed Fold - $1 Silver Certificate Series 1923**
**Portion of Oveprinted is Printed on the Back.**

**Additional Examples**

*Minor Printed Fold  - $1 FRN*
F - $50                  XF - $100                  CU - $140

*Major Foldover - $1 FRN*
F - $1,000              XF - $1,500              CU - $2,500

*Major Foldover - $1 FRN*
F - $500                XF - $1,000              CU - $1,500

*Major Tear & Foldover - $1 FRN*

F -                    XF - $1,500          CU - $3,000

*Major Double Printed Fold - $1 FRN*

F - $1,000          XF - $2,000          CU - $3,500

**Major Double Printed Fold - $1 FRN**
F - $500            XF - $1,000            CU - $1,500

**Moderate Printed Fold Affecting Back Print - $1 FRN**
F - $150            XF - $300            CU - $500

**Horizontal Fold Made Note 3/8" Higher than Normal - $1 FRN**
F - $750            XF - $1,500            CU - $2,500

*Major Tear & Foldover - $1 FRN*
F -                    XF - $1,500          CU - $3,000

*Printed Fold  - $2 FRN*
F - $750              XF - $1,500          CU - $2,500

*Huge Tear in Sheet - $2 FRN*
*Overprint on back of Center Piece was Meant for Note Below this One*
F -                    XF - $2,000        CU - $4,000

*Large Fold Affecting Face & Overprint - $5 FRN*
F - $200             XF - $400          CU - $600

*Major Printed Fold  - $5 FRN*
F - $250          XF - $500          CU - $750

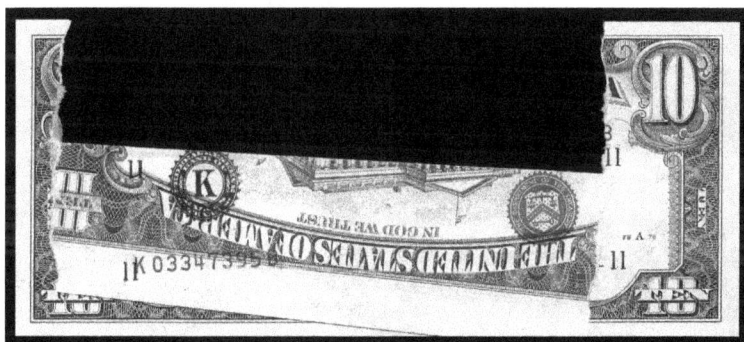

*Printed Tear Affecting Overprint - $10 FRN*
F -               XF - $1,500       CU - $3,000

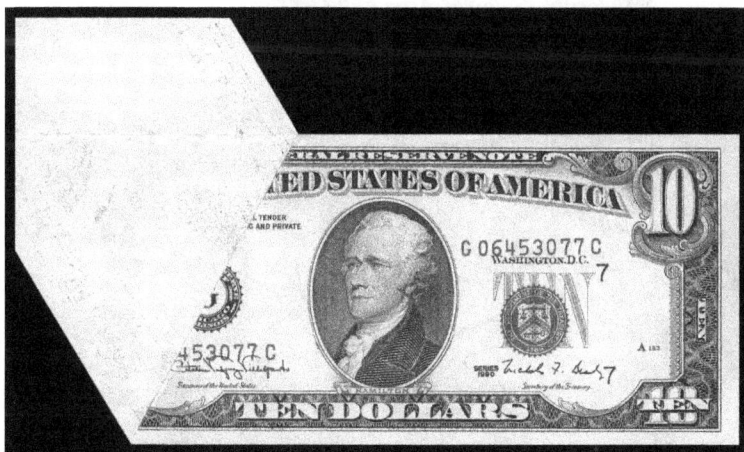

*Massive Foldover with Unprinted Face Design - $10 FRN*
F -               XF - $1,000       CU - $2,000

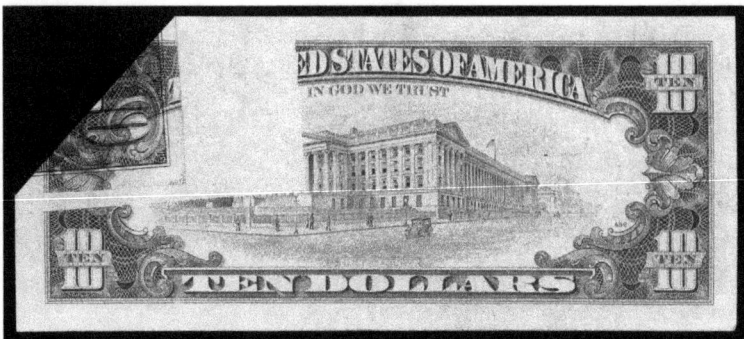

*Moderate Foldover to Back - $10 FRN*
*Missing Print is Due to Trimmed Margin and NOT Obstruction*
**F - $200          XF - $400          CU - $600**

*Moderate Foldover Affecting Overprint - $20 FRN*
**F - $200          XF - $350          CU - $500**

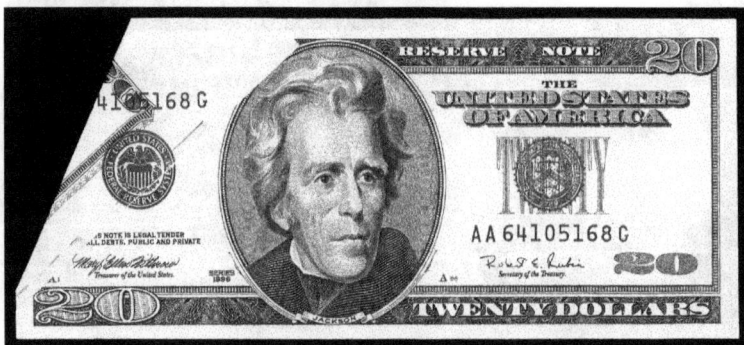

*Moderate Foldover Affecting Overprint - $20 FRN*
**F - $300          XF - $450          CU - $700**

***Massive Double Foldover  - $20 FRN***
**F -                    XF - $2,000        CU - $4,000**

***Large Foldover Affecting Back - $50 FRN***
**F - $500          XF - $750          CU - $1,000**

***Double Foldover Affecting Overprint - $50 FRN***
**F - $500          XF - $1,000        CU - $1,500**

*Major Foldover Affecting Overprint - $100 FRN*
F - $500          XF - $1,000          CU - $1,500

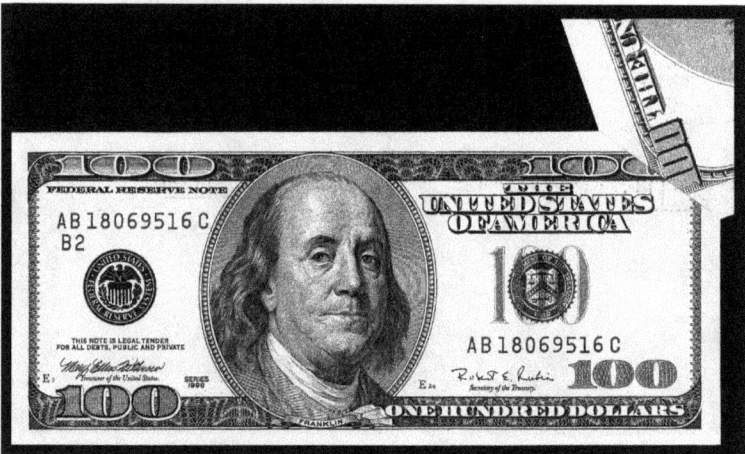

*Major Foldover Affecting Back - $100 FRN*
F - $500          XF - $1,000          CU - $1,500

*Minor Foldover Affecting Overprint - $100 FRN*
F - $150          XF - $350          CU - $750

**Readers Notes**

# Inking Errors

US currency is printed with special inks that are blended with top-secret ingredients and are meant to be virtually impossible to duplicate. Four distinct colors are used to print modern Federal Reserve Notes. The backs are printed with green ink, the faces are black and the overprint is made up of green and black ink. The inks used in the overprinting are different shades than those of the back and the face and are easily distinguished from them. A black ink smear from the face printing that has part of the black ink from the overprint on top of it will easily show the overprint ink to be different.

Security features such as Magnetic ink and color changing ink are now being used on some US currency. Problems with this ink have made some very interesting errors.

# Ink
# Smears

Ink Smears have a Class Rarity rating of R1.

Ink is delivered to the printing plates by an Ink Roller attached to an Ink Fountain. Excess ink is removed with an oscillating Wiper and a plate polisher. If the wiper blades (a type of cheese cloth) are worn, torn or fail to move across the plates, excessive ink can be deposited onto the printing plates. Excess ink can also happen if the ink jets malfunction or ink diluting solvent remains on the plates from their previous cleaning. The solvent will not allow the ink to flow into the incised design on the printing plates.

If the excess ink is not removed, it will run and smear the sheet that picks it up.

## Large Sized Currency

Minor ink Smears on Large Sized Currency are fairly rare. Moderate and Major Ink Smears are unknown.

**Note**: Ink smears can be easily counterfeited outside of the BEP. Fortunately, the ink used to print US currency is very difficult to reproduce and a note altered to represent an Ink Smear can often be easily dismissed because the colors don't look right.

The black and green inks used in the Overprinting in Federal Reserve notes are different colors than the black and green inks used for face and back printing. This may make it easier to detect a counterfeit error if the black ink of a face smear interferes with the black ink of the Overprint. The ink from the Overprint will be visible over the ink smear.

**Additional Examples**

*Major Ink Smear on Face - $1 FRN*
**F - $100          XF - $300          CU - $500**

*Minor Ink Smear on Back - $1 SC*
**F - $25          XF - $50          CU - $75**

*Minor Ink Smear of Overprint - $1 FRN*
**F - $15          XF - $25          CU - $50**

*Minor Ink Smear on Face - $2 FRN*

F - $25        XF - $50        CU - $75

*Minor Ink Smear on Back - $2 FRN*

F - $25        XF - $50        CU - $75

*Minor Ink Smear on Face - $5 FRN*

F - $25        XF - $40        CU - $55

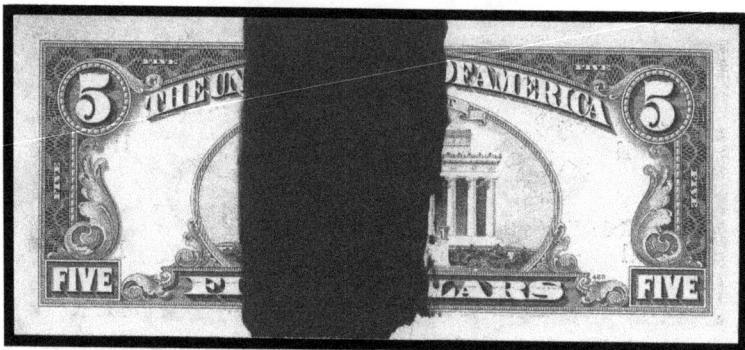

*Major Ink Smear on Back - $5 FRN*
F - $100        XF - $300        CU - $500

*Major Ink Smear on Face - $10 FRN*
F - $100        XF - $300        CU - $500

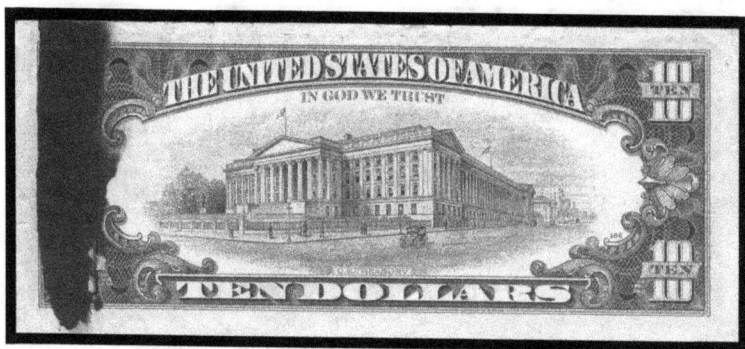

*Moderate Ink Smear on Back - $10 FRN*
F - $50        XF - $100        CU - $150

*Major Ink Smear on Face - $20 FRN*
F - $100          XF - $300          CU - $500

*Massive Ink Smear Affecting Entire Back - $20 FRN*
F - $250          XF - $500          CU - $1,000

*Major Multiple Ink Smears on Face - $50 FRN*
F - $100          XF - $200          CU - $300

*Major Multiple Ink Smears on Back - $50 FRN*
F - $100          XF - $200          CU - $300

*Moderate Ink Smear on Face - $100 FRN*
F - $150          XF - $200          CU - $350

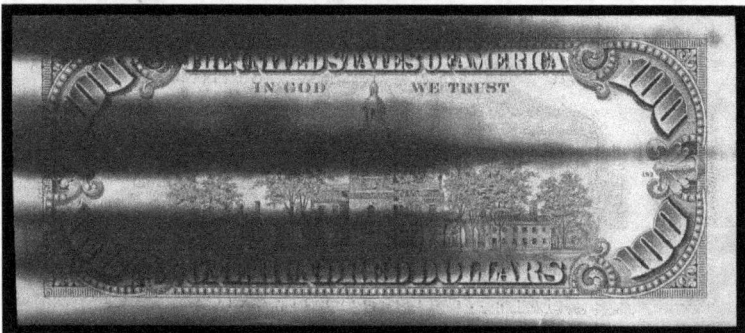

*Major Ink Smear on Back - $100 FRN*
F - $300          XF - $500          CU - $600

**Readers Notes**

# Solvent Smears

Solvent Smears have a Class Rarity rating of R1.

An ink dissolving solvent is used to clean the ink off from the printing plates after each sheet is printed. The solvent is applied to the entire printing plate and immediately wiped off with an oscillating wiper. If the wiper is worn or malfunctions or if an excess amount of solvent is applied to the plate, some of the solvent may remain on the plate and mix with the ink that is applied for the next printing. The diluted ink will cause a smear on the printing. Solvent smears differ from ink smears in that ink smears appear to contain extra ink while solvent smears appear to contain not enough or the design is simply smeared and are lighter. Telltale signs of a solvent smear may also be visible with the adjoining print appearing to run a little.

The solvent will not bleed through the currency paper. If a solvent smear appears to affect both sides of a note, the note has probably been altered after it was released from the BEP.

**Author's Note:** Solvent will not bleed through to the other side of a note. All examined examples of a double side Solvent Smear have proven to be chemically treated.

## Large Sized Currency

Solvent Smears are unknown on Large Sized Currency.

**Additional Examples**

*Moderate Solvent Smear on Face - $1 FRN*
**F - $50          XF - $150          CU - $300**

*Large Solvent Smear on Affecting Entire Back - $1 FRN*
**F - $125          XF - $250          CU - $500**

*Large Solvent Smear on Back - $1 Web Note*
**F - $250          XF - $500          CU - $1,000**

*Solvent Smear of Overprint - $1 FRN*
**F - $75          XF - $125          CU - $200**

*Moderate Solvent Smear on Face - $10 FRN*
**F - $100          XF - $150          CU - $200**

*Large Solvent Smear on Face - $20 FRN*
**F - $100          XF - $150          CU - $300**

*Massive Solvent Smear on Back - $20 FRN*
**F - $100          XF - $200          CU - $400**

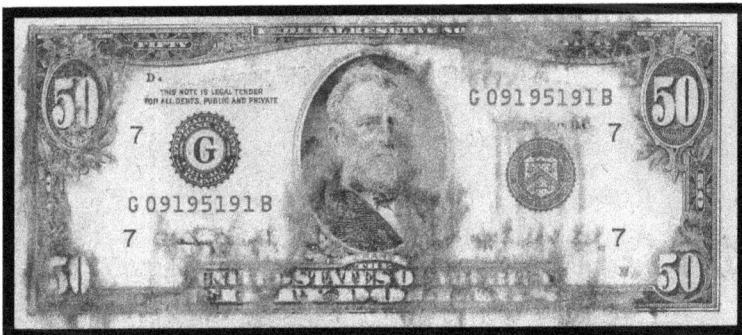

*Large Solvent Smear on Face - $50 FRN*
**F - $100          XF - $200          CU - $400**

*Moderate Solvent Smear on Face - $100 FRN*
**F - $125            XF - $200            CU - $300**

*Large Solvent Affecting Face and Color Changing Ink - $100 FRN*
**F - $150            XF - $300            CU - $600**

**Readers Notes**

# Magnetic Ink Problems

Magnetic Inking Problems have a Class Rarity rating of R5.

While magnetic ink has been both a security feature and a means of electronically identifying specific denominations of currency (bill changers and counters) for many years, changes in the magnetic ink have created an error resembling an underinked error where only portions of the face of a note are affected by the lack of ink. The underinked sections appear in a checkerboard pattern that is unique for each denomination.

This error is created when the magnetic ink does not properly adhere to the note and flakes off. It has been reported on $5, $10, $20, $50 and $100 Federal Reserve Notes from Series 1988A and later.

This error only occurs on the face of the note.

Most partial missing magnetic ink errors affect the left side of the note.

**$100 FRN with Partial Missing Magnetic Ink**

Although far less frequently found, there is no pricing difference for errors affecting the right side of the note.

**$20 FRN with Partial Missing Magnetic Ink on Right**

*Magnetic Ink Missing – Full Pattern*
**F - $250          XF - $500          CU - $1,000**

*Regular Ink Missing – Full Pattern*
**F - $500          XF - $1,500          CU - $2,500**

The Missing Ink Patterns (Checkerboard pattern) on the two previous notes are opposite because one is missing portions of the magnetic ink and one is missing portions of the regular ink.

**Additional Examples**

*Missing Magnetic Ink – Full Pattern - $5 FRN*
**F - $500          XF - $1,000          CU - $1,500**

*Missing Magnetic Ink – Full Pattern - $10 FRN*
**F - $250          XF - $500          CU - $1,000**

*Missing Magnetic Ink – Full Pattern – Light - $20 FRN*
**F - $250          XF - $500          CU - $1,000**

*Missing Magnetic Ink Missing – Partial Pattern - $20 FRN Star Note*
F - $150            XF - $400            CU - $650

*Missing Magnetic Ink- Full Pattern – New Style $20 FRN*
F - $250            XF - $500            CU - $1,000

*Missing Magnetic Ink – Partial Pattern- New Style $50 FRN*
F - $150            XF - $200            CU - $250

*Missing Magnetic Ink – Partial Pattern - $100 FRN*

**F - $150      XF - $200      CU - $250**

*Missing Magnetic Ink – Full Pattern - $100 FRN*

**F - $500      XF - $1,000      CU - $1,500**

*Missing Magnetic Ink – Partial Pattern- New Style $100 FRN*

**F - $150      XF - $200      CU - $250**

**Readers Notes**

# Under Inking

Underinked Notes have a Class Rarity Rating of R4.

Underinked notes can have a wide range of appearances. Small portions of the design can be light or missing, large sections can be completely blank, the printing can appear weak or ghostlike, or one color of the overprinting can be light or missing.

Experiments with ink and paper have been going on since the beginning of US paper money production. Some $1 notes from Series 1988 used an experimental ink that did not adhere to the paper properly and would peel and flake off along the folds and wrinkles as the note become worn. This error has not been observed on a CU note with no folds or wrinkles. Many of these notes appear to have a Board Break or Underinking error where the ink fell off from the note.

When underinking is to a point that an entire printing process (Back, Face or entire Overprint) is missing, the error is classified as a "Complete Missing Print" error (See *Complete Missing Prints* Chapter).

## Large Sized Currency

Several Large Sized Notes are known with some missing portions of print. It is unknown if these errors are the result of Board Breaks, Obstructed Prints or underinking. Many Large Sized Currency have weak or light Overprinting throughout the series. Significant Underinking Errors are unknown on Large Sized Currency.

## Underinking of Face or Back

The ink is applied to the face and back printing plates with a rubber ink roller attached to an inking fountain. The inking fountain or reservoir can become clogged or empty or the ink roller can become damaged on a small section and will not apply ink to the printing plates as the damaged area rolls across the plates.

## Insufficient Inking of Plate

When an insufficient amount of ink is applied to the printing plate from the inking roller, a gradual depletion of ink on the note is often observed. The portion of the note along the edge of the underinked section is often hazy and becomes progressively lighter.

**Gradual Depletion of Ink due to Insufficient Ink Flow**

## Progressive Underinking

Underinking due to insufficient ink is often progressive. This means that multiple notes are affected and the problem gets worse through the run of notes until either all of the ink is missing (See *Missing Prints* Chapter) or the problem is corrected (new ink is added to reservoirs).

**Progressive Underinking of Back
Ink Reservoir was Becoming Empty**

## Underinking Due to Insufficient Pressure

When the printing press is shut down, the Printing Plate Cylinder and the Impression Roller Cylinder separate as the pressure is released from them. It is still possible for a sheet of notes to continue to move a short distance through the printing process. If this sheet comes in contact with the inked printing plates, it will pick up some of the ink from this plate. There will not be enough pressure to force the ink from the cuts of the plate onto the paper but enough of the ink can be picked up to easily identify what the design should have been. This can affect the entire sheet but most often only affects a small portion (therefore only affecting a few notes on the sheet.)

When the press is shut down in the middle of a printing run, some of the design will be correctly printed and some can be light and hazy. The separation line between the inked areas and the underinked (or uninked) areas is always horizontal.

**Major Underinking due to Insufficient Pressure**

## Underinking of Overprint

The Overprint presses are fed ink from an inking fountain or reservoir. As this reservoir becomes empty or clogged, the Overprinting can get lighter or disappear altogether. Notes with two color Overprints never have both colors affected at the same time. On Modern Federal Reserve Notes, more green ink is used in the overprinting than black ink. The inking reservoirs are the same size so if unattended, the green would require refilling sooner. When the black ink was depleted, the previously refilled green ink reservoir would still contain sufficient ink.

Series 1928B and 1934 Federal Reserve Notes printed with both dark and light green seals. The light green seal often looks yellow-green. Both types of this note are available to collectors but neither is an inking problem.

**Underinking of Black Ink in Overprint**

**Additional Examples of Underinked Back Errors**

*Underinking of Back - $1 FRN*
F - $75          XF - $125          CU - $250

*Partial Underinking of Back- Strong Delineation - $1 FRN*
F - $75          XF - $125          CU - $250

*Underinking of Back - $5 FRN*
F - $75          XF - $125          CU - $250

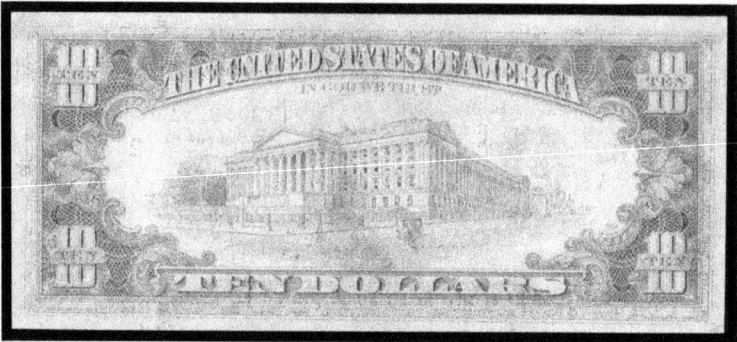

*Underinking of Back - $10 FRN*

F - $75          XF - $125          CU - $250

*Partial Underinking of Back - $1 FRN*

F - $75          XF - $125          CU - $250

*Underinking of Back - $20 FRN*

F - $250          XF - $500          CU - $750

*Partial Underinking of Back - $50 FRN*
F - $75          XF - $100          CU - $150

*Underinking of Back - $100 FRN*
F - $250          XF - $500          CU - $750

*Partial Underinking of Back – Strong Delineation - $100 FRN*
F - $125          XF - $250          CU - $500

**Additional Examples of Underinked Face Errors**

*Partial Underinking of Face - $1 FRN*

F - $100          XF - $200          CU - $300

*Underinking of Face - $1 FRN*

F - $250          XF - $500          CU - $750

*Gradual Underinking of Face - $1 FRN*

F - $100          XF - $250          CU - $500

**Underinking of Face - $5 FRN**
F - $250          XF - $500          CU - $750

**Gradual Underinking of Face - $5 FRN**
F - $100          XF - $250          CU - $500

**Underinking of Face - $10 FRN**
F - $250          XF - $500          CU - $750

**Underinking of Face - $20 FRN**
F - $250            XF - $500            CU - $750

**Partial Underinking of Face - Strong Delineation - $50 FRN**
F - $500            XF - $1,000            CU - $1,500

**Underinking of Face - $100 FRN**
F - $250            XF - $750            CU - $1,000

**Additional Examples of Underinked Overprint Errors**

*Underinking of Black Overprint  - $1 FRN*
**F - $25            XF - $50            CU - $75**

*Underinking of Green Oveprint  - $1 FRN*
**F - $50            XF - $125            CU - $250**

*Underinking of Black Overprint  - $2 FRN*
**F - $50            XF - $75            CU - $100**

*Underinking of Green Oveprint - $5 FRN*

**F - $50            XF - $100            CU - $200**

*Underinking of Single Digit in Serial Numbers  - $5 FRN*

**F - $40            XF - $75            CU - $125**

*Underinking of Magnetic Ink - $100 FRN*

**F -            XF - $125            CU - $150**

**Readers Notes**

# Wrong
# Color Ink

Wrong Color Ink Errors have a Class Rarity Rating of R9.

Occasionally a note will be found with ink in the overprint that is not the right color. Federal Reserve Notes have been discovered bearing overprints printed with a mixture of both the black and green inks found in the overprints and with overprints that were printed with the wrong color ink altogether.

Ink is added to the overprint reservoirs manually. In overprinting, the black & green ink are both used and they are stored in the same area.

This error is only found in the overprint. No note has ever been documented with a contaminated Ink of the face or back. Face and back printings are done in different areas so the other color of inks is not easily accessible when printing one side or the other.

Black and green ink are sometimes mixed to get a *brownish* or *reddish* color.

Most notes that have the portion of the overprint that is usually green printed in yellowish ink are altered by adding bleach (accidentally washing the note) to the note. The green inks used in the overprinting and the back printing can be turned yellow or blue with the addition of an alkali or an acidic solution.

**Author's Note:** There have been several new-style notes that have surfaced with bright-blue ink in place of the green ink in the overprint. All examples of this error that I have personally examined are suspected alterations.

## Large Sized Currency

Wrong Color Ink errors are extremely rare on Large Sized Currency.

### Known Examples

| Denom / Type | Series | Fr No. | Serial Number | Grade |
|---|---|---|---|---|
| $100 / GC | 1922 | Fr 1215 | N2385266 | XF |
| Seal that should be Red is printed with same color Gold ink used to print the word "GOLD" on the front of the note. | | | | |

**Wrong Ink Color Used for Seal - $100 GC Series 1922**

## Additional Examples

*District Seal and District Letters Printed*
*with Green Ink Instead of Black*
**F - $250        XF - $500        CU - $1,000**

*District Seal and District Letters Printed*
*with Green Ink Instead of Black*
**F - $250        XF - $500        CU - $1,000**

*District Seal and District Letters Printed*
*with Green Ink Instead of Black*
**F - $250        XF - $500        CU - $1,000**

**Readers Notes**

# Missing Prints

Many things can go wrong during the printing processes that can prevent notes from receiving the entire design that is meant to be printed. This section discusses Missing Prints resulting from a breakdown of the impression cylinder (See *Board Breaks* Chapter), foreign obstructions (See *Obstructed Prints* Chapter) and printings that are completely missing, no matter what the cause (See *Complete Missing Prints* Chapter).

Missing prints can also occur due to folds and tears (See *Folds and Tears* Chapter) and inking problems (See *Underinking* Chapter).

# Board
# Breaks

Board Breaks have a Class Rarity rating of R6.

A high amount of pressure is used to press the paper onto the printing plates. A hard surface used as a pressing agent would quickly crack the printing cylinder so an impression cylinder is used. Multiple layers of sheets of heavy fiberboard covered with a rubber coating cover the impression cylinder.

These fiberboards are often called "Rigging" or "Batting" boards. This cardboard eventually cracks, peels and compresses under the extreme pressure, leaving blank areas where little or no pressure is put onto the paper. The missing design on the paper is called a Board Break.

## Large Sized Currency

Board Breaks are unknown on Large Sized Currency.

**Additional Examples**

*Massive Board Break - $1 FRN*
*This same Board Break is Known on Notes from*
*3 Different Districts and on a Star Note*
F - $150          XF - $300          CU - $450

*Large Diagonal Board Break - $1 FRN*
F - $100          XF - $200          CU - $300

*Moderate Board Break at Top of Face - $1FRN*
**F - $50          XF - $100          CU - $150**

*Massive Board Break - $1 FRN*
**F - $150          XF - $300          CU - $450**

*Moderate Board Break - $1 FRN*
**F - $50          XF - $100          CU - $150**

**Board Breaks at Top of Face - $2 FRN**
F - $100          XF - $200          CU - $300

**Massive Board Break - $10 FRN**
F - $150          XF - $300          CU - $450

**Board Break at Bottom Left of Face - $20 FRN**
F - $75          XF - $110          CU - $150

**Readers Notes**

# Obstructed Prints

Obstructed Prints have a Class Rarity Rating of R5.

Obstructed Prints with the Obstruction retained with the note are discussed in the following Chapter.

An Obstructed Print error is caused when something comes in contact with an unprinted portion of a sheet of notes and remains intact during the printing process. Such obstructions can be caused by practically anything that can be brought into the BEP. More often than not, the obstruction is a portion of a sheet of currency or a piece of the wide margins that were trimmed. A few of the extremely rare examples include obstructions from a Band-Aid tab, a cellophane wrapper from a cigarette pack and a Del Monte banana sticker.

When the obstruction is part of the note itself due to a fold, it is classified as a Paper Fold error.

Obstructions nearly always cause a very sharp delineation line between the printed section and the blank area. Gradual fading of ink along the delineation line often point to another cause of missing ink such as underinking (See *Under Inking* chapter), excess Solvent (See *Solvent Smear* chapter) or a Board Break (See *Board Break* chapter).

When the obstruction remains with the note, it is called a Retained Obstruction error (See *Retained Obstruction* Chapter).

## Large Sized Currency

Obstructed Prints on Large Sized Currency are rare. Several Series of Large Sized Currency were printed with multi-colored faces that required several inking passes. Obstructions of only one of these colors make very eye appealing errors. The Obstruction of part of the overprint is the most common obstruction error found on Large Sized Currency.

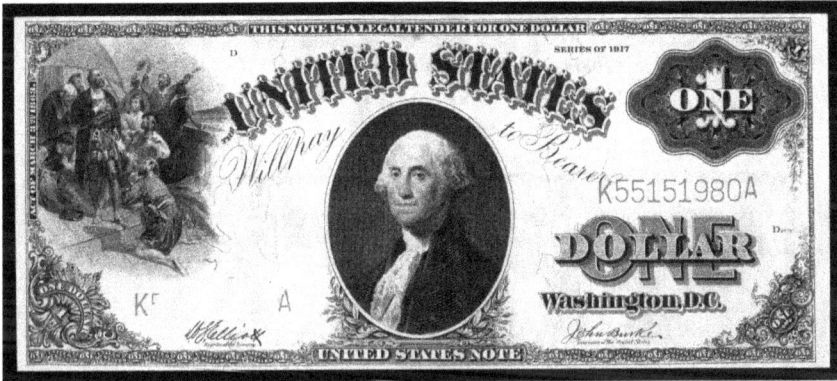

**Obstruction of Right Serial Number**
**F - $600          XF - $800          CU - $1000**

**Obstruction of One Color of Multi-Colored Face**
**F - $700          XF - $900          CU - $1100**

**Additional Examples**

*Obstruction of Face Design - $1 FRN*
F - $100          XF - $150          CU - $200

*Minor Obstruction of Back Design - $1 SC*
F - $50          XF - $75          CU - $100

*Obstruction of Overprint – Black Portion Only - $1 FRN*
F - $100          XF - $200          CU - $400

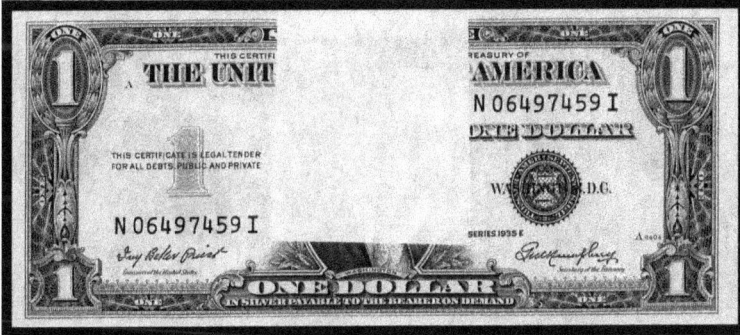

*Major Obstruction of Face Design - $1 SC*
F - $250          XF - $500          CU - $750

*Minor Obstruction of Face Design - $5 FRN*
F - $100          XF - $150          CU - $200

*Major Obstruction of Back Design - $5 FRN*
F - $250          XF - $500          CU - $750

*Obstruction of Overprint – Black Portion Only – $5 FRN*
**F - $100                XF - $200                CU - $400**

*Obstruction Caused by Punched Paper from Alignment Hole*
*Early 18 subject sheets of paper had a series of alignment holes punched along both sides. These holes were used to guide the sheets into the printing processes and maintain their alignment. It is speculated that the holes were used to eliminate alignment problems that might have sprung from the use of a larger (and possibly harder to handle) sheet of paper.*
**F - $50                XF - $100                CU - $200**

***Obstruction of Overprint – Black Portion Only - $10 FRN***
**F - $100          XF - $200          CU - $400**

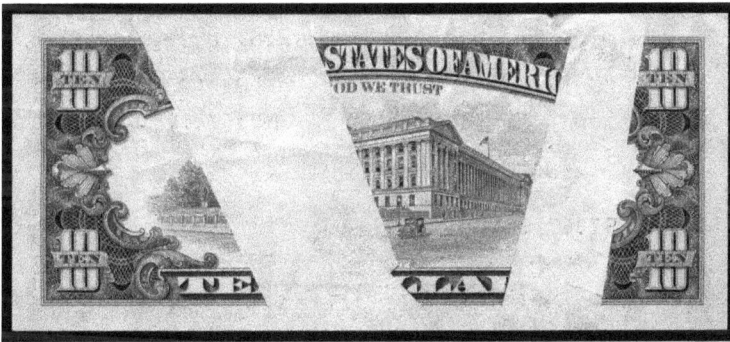

***Multiple Obstructions of Back Design - $10 FRN***
**F - $250          XF - $500          CU - $750**

***Moderate Obstruction of Face Design - $20 FRN***
**F - $150          XF - $300          CU - $400**

*Obstruction of Overprint - $20 FRN*

**F - $100          XF - $200          CU - $400**

*Minor Obstruction of Face Design - $50 FRN*

**F - $150          XF - $200          CU - $250**

*Obstruction of Back Design - $100 FRN*

**F - $250          XF - $500          CU - $1,000**

**Readers Notes**

# Retained Obstructions

Retained Obstructions have a Class Rarity Rating of R9.

A Retained Obstructed error is caused when something comes in contact with an unprinted portion of a sheet of notes, remains intact during the printing and cutting process, and is discovered with the note outside of the BEP. Such obstructions can be caused by practically anything that can be brought into the BEP. More often than not, the obstruction is a portion of a sheet of currency or a piece of the wide margins that were trimmed. A few of the extremely rare examples include obstructions from a Band-Aid tab, a cellophane wrapper from a cigarette pack, portions of sizing sheets used to separate the stacks of paper as they are printed, and a Del Monte banana sticker.

## Large Sized Currency

There are no known examples of Obstructed Print with Retained Obstruction on Large Sized Currency.

**Additonal Examples**

*Retained Obstruction – Brown Kraft Paper*
F -                    XF - $5,000        CU - $7,500

*Retained Obstruction – Currency Stock – Trimmed Margin*
F -                    XF - $5,000        CU - $7,500

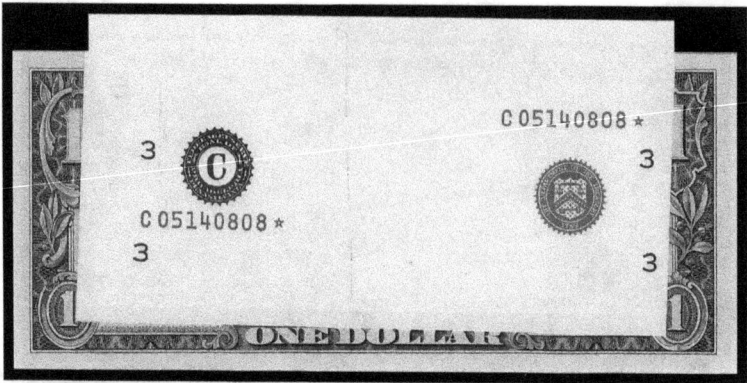

**Retained Obstructionon Star Note  – Sizing Sheet**
**The Sizing Sheet has since Been Separted from this Note**
F -                    XF - $7,500        CU - $15,000

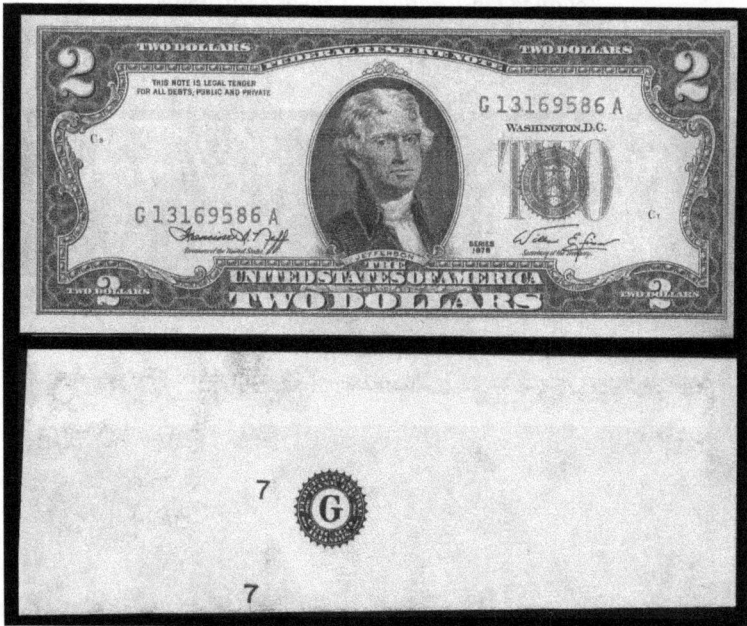

**Retained Obstruction – Thick Yellow Paper**
**Obstruction Occurred between Green and Black Portions of the Oveprint**
F -                    XF - $7,500        CU - $15,000

*Retained Obstruction – 3 Separate Pieces of Currency Stock*
**F -                    XF - $7,500        CU - $10,000**

*Retained Obstruction – Currency Stock*
**F -                    XF - $7,500        CU - $15,000**

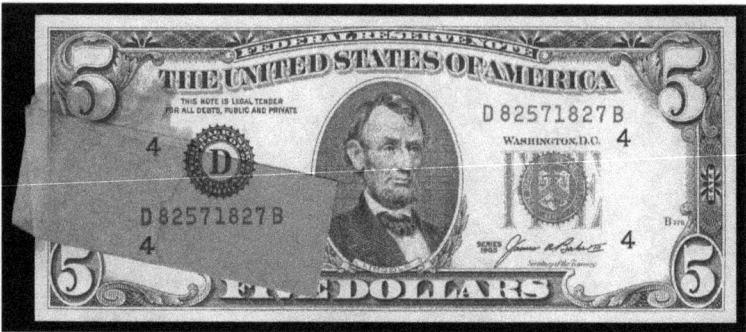

*Retained Obstruction – Brown Kraft Paper & Masking Tape*
F -                   XF - $5,000        CU - $7,500

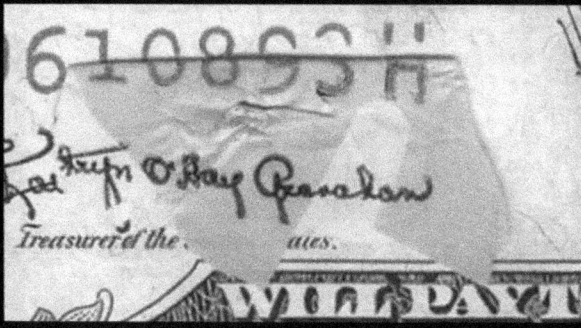

*Retained Obstruction – Green Cellophane*
F -                   XF - $5,000        CU - $7,500

*Retained Obstruction – Brown Kraft Paper & Masking Tape*
**F -              XF - $5,000        CU - $7,500**

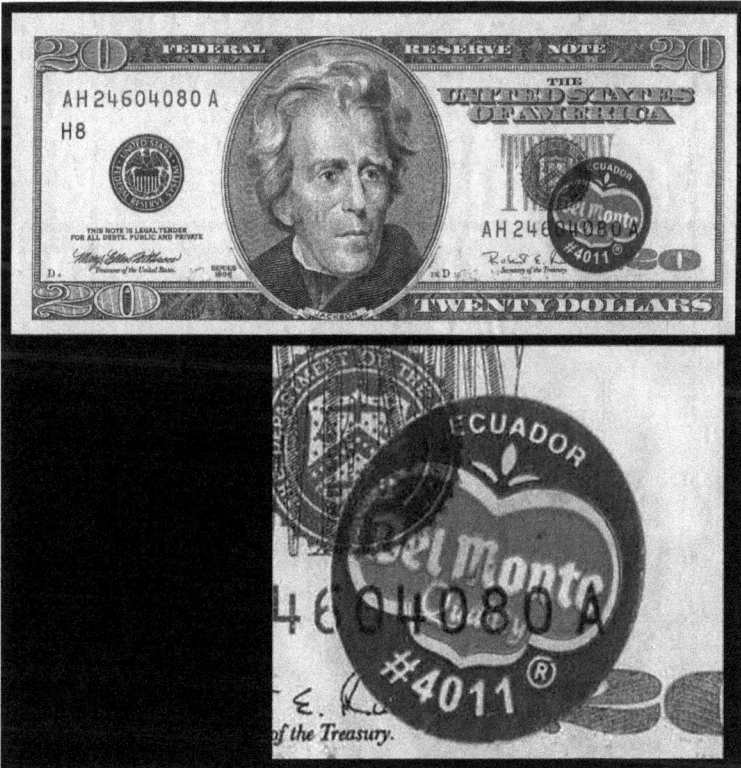

*Retained Obstruction – Del Monte Banaa Stickerr*
**F -              XF - $7,500        CU - $15,000**

***Retained Obstruction – Batting Cloth***

F -                     XF - $5,000          CU - $7,500

***Retained Obstruction – Brown Kraft Paper***

F -                     XF - $6,000          CU - $9,000

## Readers Notes

# Complete Missing Prints

US Currency is printed in 3 different processes; Back printing (1st Printing), Face printing (2nd Printing) and Overprinting (3rd Printing). This chapter deals with the errors that are created when all of one of these printings is missing.

Complete Missing Print errors are created in a variety of ways.

- Two sheets can adhere together and pass through the printing press at the same time, leaving one side of one of the sheets unprinted.

- A sheet can have a major foldover prior to one of its printings. The fold must be large enough to affect the entire design of at least one note on the sheet.

- A printing operation can be skipped completely. Pallets of notes are moved from printing operation to printing operation and are left to dry in special drying rooms (often) overnight. It is possible for a pallet of notes to be moved to the wrong *next operation*, skipping an entire printing process.

- Underinking of printing plates to the point where no ink is delivered to the plates at all.

## Missing Back Print

Missing Back Prints have a Class Rarity Rating of R6.

These errors are commonly referred to as "Blank Back" notes.

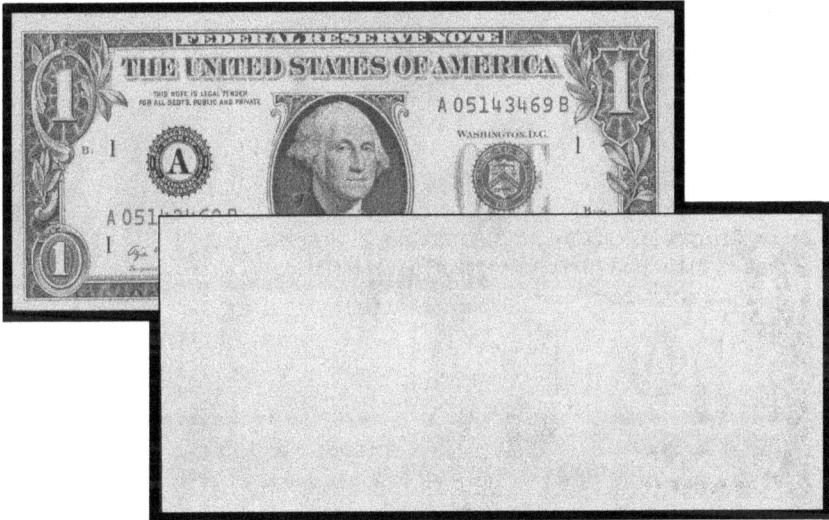

**Missing Back Printing - $1 FRN**

## Large Sized Currency

No "Blank Back" errors have been  recorded on Large Sized Currency.

## Additional Examples

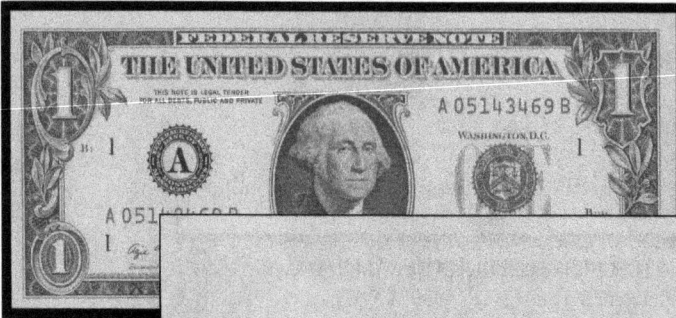

*Blank Back - $1 FRN*

**F - $175          XF - $350          CU - $700**

*Blank Back - $5 FRN*

**F - $175          XF - $350          CU - $700**

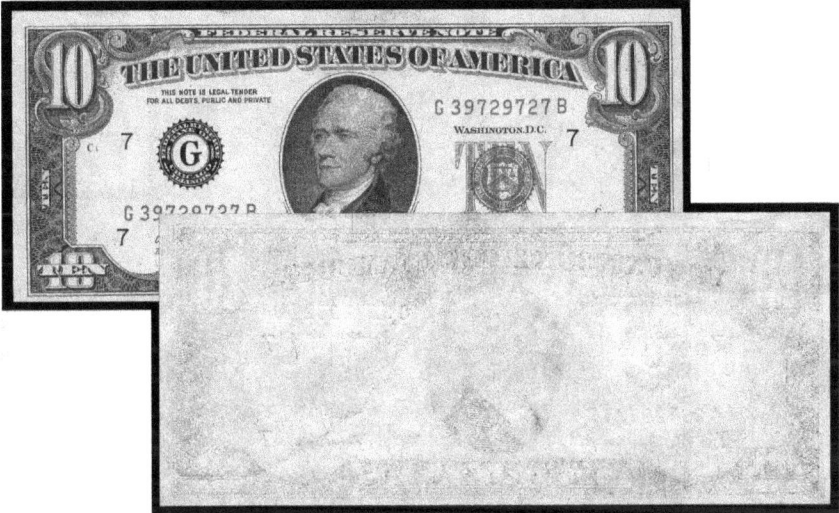

*Blank Back - $10 FRN*
F - $175          XF - $350          CU - $700

*Blank Back - $20 FRN*
F - $175          XF - $350          CU - $700

*Blank Back - $50 FRN*

**F - $500          XF - $1,000          CU - $2,000**

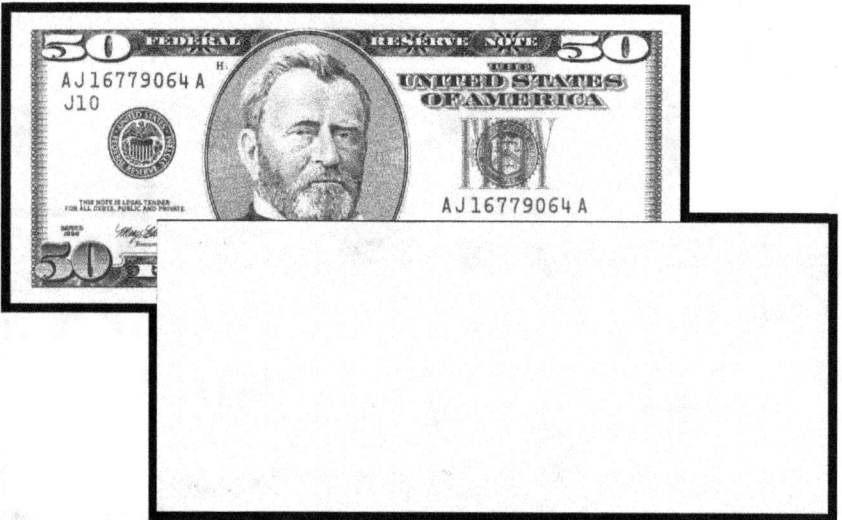

*Blank Back – New Style $50 FRN*

**F - $500          XF - $1,000          CU - $2,000**

*Blank Back - $100 FRN*
**F - $500          XF - $1,000          CU - $2,000**

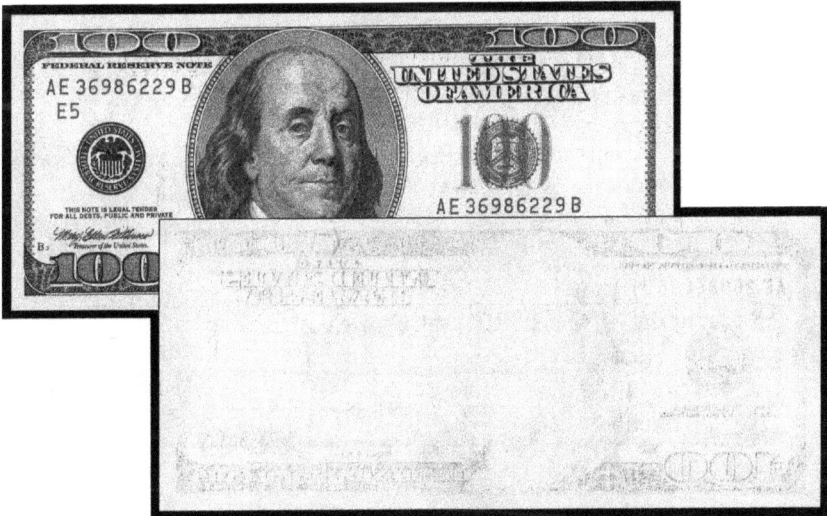

*Blank Back – New Style $100 FRN*
**F - $750          XF - $1,500          CU - $2,500**

## Missing Face Print

Missing Face Prints have a Class Rarity Rating of R8.

**Missing Face Printing - $1 FRN**

## Large Sized Currency

There are only two recorded examples of the Missing Face Printing Error on Large Sized Currency.

| Denom. | Series | Fr. No. | Serial Number | Grade |
|--------|--------|---------|---------------|-------|
| $10 | LT | 1862 | Fr ? | None | **VF** |
| No face printing. Green "10"s and Ornate design is only printing On face. | | | | |
| $500 | GC | 1882 | Fr ? | None | **VF** |
| No face printing. Gold Overprint is only printing on face. | | | | |

## Additional Examples

*Missing Face Printing - $1 FRN*
**F - $500          XF - $1,000          CU - $1,500**

*Missing Face Printing - $5 FRN*
**F - $500          XF - $1,000          CU - $1,500**

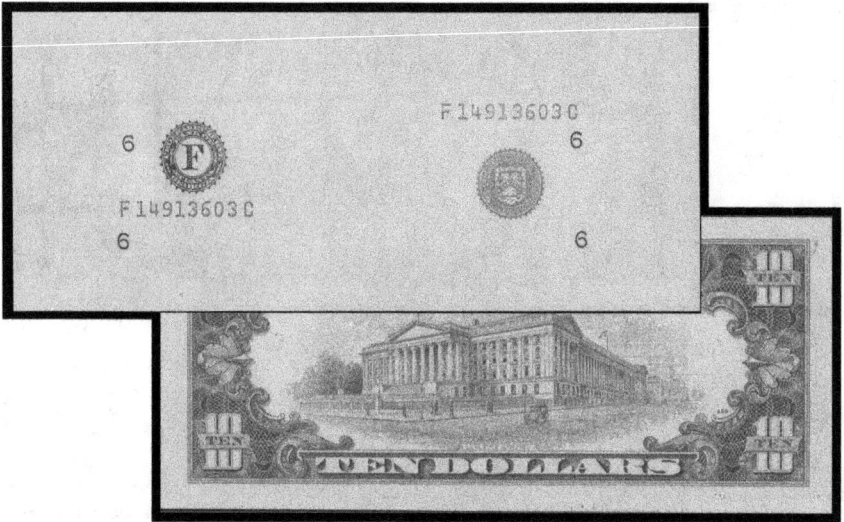

***Missing Face Printing - $10 FRN***
**F - $500          XF - $1,000          CU - $1,500**

***Missing Face Printing - $20 FRN***
**F - $500          XF - $1,000          CU - $1,500**

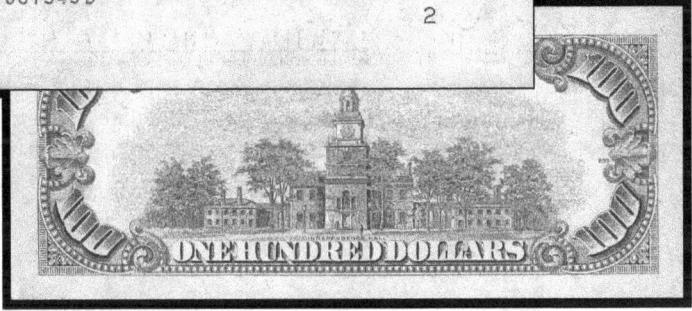

*Missing Face Printing - $100 FRN*
**F - $1,000          XF - $2,000          CU - $3,000**

*Missing Face Printing - $100 FRN- New Style*
**F - $1,000          XF - $2,000          CU - $3,000**

## Missing Overprint

Missing Overprints have a Class Rarity Rating of R7.

**Missing Overprint - $1 FRN**

Although the overprinting on modern currency is often called the "third print", that is not really true. The green and black portions of the overprinting are printed in different steps (although done in the same machine). A note that is completely missing one color of the overprint also falls into this category.

## Large Sized Currency

Numerous Examples of Missing Overprints have been recorded on Large Sized Currency.

**Author's Note:** A large number of Large Sized Notes Missing the overprint that I have personally examined are suspected alterations. I once saw an entire collection of these notes where each individual note had been framed and hung on the wall of the office of the collector. Years of sunlight exposure had caused the overprints to fade away completely.

**Additional Examples**

*Missing Oveprint - $1 SC*
F - $500            XF - $750            CU - $1,000

*Missing Overprint - $1 FRN*
F - $100            XF - $250            CU - $400

*Missing Green Portion of Overprint - $1 FRN*
F - $100            XF - $250            CU - $400

*Missing Black Portion of Overprint - $1 FRN*
**F - $100              XF - $250              CU - $400**

*Missing Overprint - $2FRN*
**F - $2,000          XF - $4,000          CU - $8,000**

*Missing Overprint - $5 FRN*
**F - $100              XF - $250              CU - $400**

*Missing Overprint – Early $10 FRN*
*The Black District Seals and Numbers were Part of the Face Print*
**F - $1,000          XF - $3,000          CU - $5,000**

*Missing Overprint - $10 FRN*
**F - $100          XF - $250          CU - $400**

*Missing Overprint - $20 FRN*
**F - $150          XF - $250          CU - $500**

*Missing Overprint - $50 FRN*

F - $400          XF - $800          CU - $1,200

*Missing Overprint – New Style $50 FRN*

F - $500          XF - $1,000          CU - $1,500

*Missing Overprint – New Style $100 FRN*
*The Universal District Seals is Part of the Face Print*

F - $500          XF - $1,000          CU - $1,500

**Readers Notes**

# Overprinting Errors

Overprinting is often referred to as the 3rd printing but this can be misleading. Overprinting is defined as anything that is printed on the notes after the back and face prints are completed. This is currently the Serial Numbers, Treasury Seal and District Seal and numbers. In the past, the overprint included the word "HAWAII" printed twice on the face and once on the back, National Bank information, Treasurer and Registers signatures and Bank Official signatures and printings on the face and back of some fractional currency. Some of these processes required a 4th and 5th printing.

The Serial Numbers that are printed in the overprinting process do not index upwardly Starting at A00000001A and ending with A00020000A in the First Plate position of the first complete run of notes. Instead, they index downwardly so that the last sheet to receive the overprint will be the lowest number and also be the top sheet of the pallet.

COPE-PAK is an acronym for Currency Overprinting and Processing Equipment and Packaging. These machines apply the green and black overprints to half sheets of modern US Currency.

The COPE-PAK machines are equipped with 32 separate numbering machines. Each numbering machine contains two numbering blocks that will apply the two serial numbers to the notes. Each of the numbering blocks acts independently from the others and has to be set manually to the desired serial number at the start of each run.

These blocks can be set incorrectly or can jam or clog during production runs.

The COPE-PAK machines are equipped with automatic scanning systems. These systems check for these problems with the Serial Numbering machines. When a problem is encountered, the systems are supposed to shut down the printing press and alert the pressman to the exact problem.

This chapter discusses errors that are encountered during the Overprinting process. Obstructed Serial numbers (see *Obstructed Prints* Chapter), Missing Serial Numbers (See *Underinking* and *Complete Missing Prints* Chapter) and alignment problems (See *Alignment* Section) are covered in different sections of this book.

# Identical Serial Numbers on Same Series and Denomination Notes

The Serial Numbers on US currency are the key feature in labeling each note as unique. These numbers have been used to assist in the identification of stolen money, known counterfeits and evaluations of length of time in circulation for BEP wear and durability tests. These numbers are also used by the numismatic community to track known grades and sales prices.

No two notes from the same series and denomination are supposed to have the same serial numbers. Such an occurrence would have been grounds for imprisonment 100 years ago and possibly death 200 years ago.

Electronic equipment attached to the COPE-PAK machines monitor the activity of each set of numbering blocks. When the numbering blocks fail, the sensors automatically shut down the overprinting press and pinpoint the problem for the press operator to fix.

Identical Serial Numbers on the same series and denomination of notes can occur when both numbering blocks fail to advance. When only one block does not advance, the note affected note will have mismatched serial numbers.

**Caution:** The notes are only considered errors when they are from the same series and denomination. There are many examples of notes with the same serial numbers but from different series on the marketplace. While these notes are considered novelties they are not errors.

**Reported Examples**

| Denom \| Type | Date | Serial Number |
|---|---|---|
| $1 \| FRN | 1969D | B 33930780 C[1] |
| $1 \| FRN | 1981 | L 95837284 C |

1 - The bookend notes with Serial Numbers ending in 779 C and 782 C were also kept with the error notes. The serial numbers of the notes suggest that the sheet bearing Serial Numbers ending in 781 C was pulled instead of the second sheet ending in Serial numbers 780 C.

**Additional Examples**

*Same Denomination, Series and Serial Numbers*
**F -          XF - $6,000        CU - $12,000**

**Readers Notes**

# Improperly Indexed Serial Numbers

The first 3 digits of the serial number (after the prefix) are locked in place and aren't supposed to move during the overprinting process. When the serial number of the last sheet indexes to the next 100,000, the note will have a zero instead of a one in the third digit of the serial number.

**Known Examples**

| Denom \| Type | Date | Serial Number |
|---|---|---|
| $1 \| FRN | 1963 | A 00000000 A[1] |
| $5 \| FRN | 1950-C | F 27000000 C |

[1] – Could have been either Serial Number A10000000A or A00100000A. Either number would have produced the same solid zero serial number.

**Additional Examples**

*Improperly Indexed Serial Number - $5 FRN*
**F -            XF - $7,500        CU - $10,000**

**Readers Notes**

# Misaligned / Rolled Digits

Misaligned Digits have a Class Rarity rating of R2.

Rolled Digits have a Class Rarity rating of R4.

The Serial Numbers on US Currency are printed by two separate numbering blocks. Each block is made up of several numbering wheels. These wheels contain the letters and the numbers that make up the serial numbers.

Serial numbering wheels act the same way as the odometer in a car except the numbers decrease. Each time the numbering wheel indexes to 0, it turns the next dial to the next *lower* number (the wheels index downward, instead of upward because the printing order of the serial numbers is from highest to lowest). Occasionally the dial will clog with dust or ink and fail to operate properly.

Digit Alignment Errors are separated into two distinct categories. A Misaligned Digit error has one or more digits that are out of alignment with the others by at least 25%. A Rolled Digit error occurs when the digit in question is do far out of alignment that either a portion of it is not printed or it displays portions of two different digits. Rolled digits are sometimes referred to as Stuck Digit, Turned Digit or Gas Pump errors.

**Misaligned Digit**          **Rolled Digit**

## Large Sized Currency

Misaligned Digits on Large Sized Currency are fairly common and command no premium as an error note. Rolled digit errors on Large Sized Currency are extremely rare.

**Additional Examples**

*Rolled Digit - $1 SC*

**F - $50**            **XF - $100**            **CU - $200**

*Misaligned Digit - $1 FRN*

**F - $5**            **XF - $10**            **CU - $20**

*Rolled Digit - $1 FRN Star Note*
**F - $250            XF - $500            CU - $750**

*Rolled Digit - $1 FRN With Multiple Rolled Digits*
**F - $500            XF - $750            CU - $1,000**

*Misaligned Digit - $2 FRN*

**F - $10                    XF - $20                    CU - $40**

*Rolled Digit - $2 LT*

**F - $500                    XF - $1,000                    CU - $1,500**

*Rolled Digit - $5 FRN*

**F - $25                    XF - $50                    CU - $100**

***Rolled Digit in Suffix - $10 FRN***
**F - $25              XF - $50              CU - $100**

***Rolled Digit - $10 NC***
**F - $1,000          XF - $3,000          CU - $5,000**

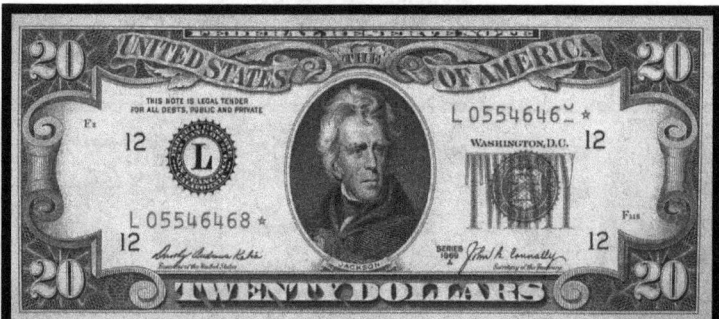

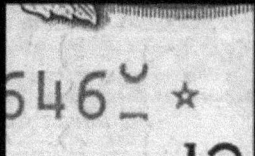

***Rolled Digit - $20 FRN Star Note***
**F - $250            XF - $500            CU - $750**

**Readers Notes**

# Mismatched Serial Numbers

Mismatched Serial Numbers have a Class Rarity Rating of R5.

Serial Numbers are applied to modern US Currency by numbering machines attached to the overprinting equipment. Each numbering machine contains two numbering blocks that will apply the two serial numbers to the notes. Each of the numbering blocks acts independently from the others and has to be set manually to the desired serial number to start each run. The first three digits are locked into place are not supposed to move. The last five digits index for every note that is printed. Modern notes are printed in runs of 10,000 and 20,000 sheets and do not require the first three digits to index.

When the two numbering blocks are accidentally set to different numbers prior to the printing run, or when one numbering block jams or clogs during production runs, a note with Mismatched Serial Numbers is created.

Mismatches almost always occur in one single position on a printed sheet. The sheet position is always the same for runs of these mismatches. There is only one documented example of two mismatched serial number notes coming from the same sheet.

A Single digit mismatch can appear to be a multiple digit mismatch when the numbers go into different 10's (100's, etc.). XXXXXX09 and XXXXXX10 are only one number apart but the error is often classified as a double digit mismatch. There are several examples of XXXX9999 and XXX10000 type mismatches.

The majority of mismatches occur with the serial numbers differing by the same number of digits, but a few known runs are known when one of the Serial Numbering blocks fails to advance while the other block continues to work properly.

**This Note Displays the Correct Matching Serial Numbers**

**The Right Serial Numbering Block Froze**
**But the Left Serial Number Continued to Advance Properly**

**Author's Note:** There's been some press lately about the rarity of two mismatched serial numbered notes with the same serial number appearing once on both notes. These notes are ***not*** any rarer than their counterparts. Several runs of mismatches are known where one serial number froze in place making large runs of these errors have the same serial number on multiple notes. Also, a one digit mismatch at the end of a serial number will have the same serial number on ***every*** pair of consecutive notes (Serial Number A0123456[7|8]A and the next note, Serial Number A0123456[8|9]A will have A01234568A appearing on both notes. The same thing would happen for the next note and so on.

## Large Sized Currency

Mismatched Serial Numbers on Large Sized Currency are extremely rare.

**Known Examples**

| Denom. \| Type | Series | Fr No. | Serial Number[1] |
|---|---|---|---|
| $1 \| US | 1862 | Fr 16 | 408[63\|57][2] |
| | | | 8382[2\|6] |
| | 1869 | Fr 18 | Z 8203[67\|71] ★ |
| | 1917 | Fr 37 | H 654[0\|1]0001 A |
| | | Fr 39 | R 2251478[7\|9] A[3] |
| | | | R 2251479[1\|3] A[3] |
| $1 \| SC | 1899 | Fr 228 | R 78755[400\|398] |
| | | Fr 233 | D 1150[6\|7]050 A |
| | | | D 3847[7\|6]001 A |
| | 1923 | Fr 237 | B 68073[098\|102] D |
| $2 \| US | 1862 | Fr 41 | 9[0\|6]890 |
| $5 \| SC | 1899 | Fr 278 | M 8276235[8\|4] |
| $5 \| NC | 1902 | | 1[1\|0]200 |
| First NB, Sabina, OH. Charter #8411 | | | |

[1] - The Serial Numbers are listed with the mismatched digit(s) in brackets. The digits on the left side correspond to the left serial number and the digits on the right side correspond to the right serial number. The listing 408[63|57] would have Serial Number 40863 on the left and Serial Number 40657 on the right.

[2] - This Serial Number combination was mislisted as 408[53|57] in an auction catalog and has since been mislisted in the error note sections of several paper money references. The Serial Numbers listed here are the actual Serial Numbers appearing on the note.

[3] - Early US currency was printed on sheets that contained consecutively numbered notes. It is impossible to find consecutive Mismatched Serial Number notes in Series that were printed on these sheets. These two notes are consider consecutive errors as they were from consecutive sheets and are from the same plate position.

## Mismatched Serial Numbers

**Known Examples**

| Denom \| Type | Series | Serial Number[1] |
|---|---|---|
| $1 \| SC | 1934 | A 8[4\|3]2XXXXX A |
| | | D XXXXXX[0\|1]X A |
| | 1935A | I 152[0\|1]XXXX B |
| | | T 302XXX[3\|7]X C |
| | | X 679XXXX[1\|0] B |
| | | Y 024XXX[1\|0]X B |
| | 1935C | P 374X[4009\|393] D |
| | | T 00[9\|0]XXXXX D[2] |
| | 1935D | B073[1\|0]XXXX F |
| | | B 153XXX[0\|1]X G |
| | | G [7\|6]77XXXXX G |
| | | K 697[5\|6]XXXX G |
| | | W 635XXX[6\|5]X F |
| | | X 382XXX[0\|1]X F |
| | 1935E | A [1\|2]93XXXXX H |
| | | A 436XXX[XX\|70] H[3] |
| | | A 880XXXX[0\|1] H |
| | | D 535XXXX[0\|1] I |
| | | F 8[4\|6]2XXXXX I |
| | | G [25\|14]2XXXXX H |
| | | N 647XXXX[3\|0] H[4] |
| | | R 105[2\|3]XXXX G |
| | | S 197XX[001\|142] H |
| | | X 5[3\|4]8XXXXX G |
| | | Y [3\|2]85XXXX[0\|9] [ ■ \|G][5] |
| | | Z 16[0\|1]XXXXX G |
| | | ★ 3[5\|4]6XXXXX D |
| | 1935F | ★ 655XXX[1\|0]X F |
| | 1935G | D 466XXX[1\|0]X J |
| | | ★ 182XXXX[2\|0] G |

| Denom | Type | Series | Serial Number[1] |
|---|---|---|
| $1 | SC | 1957 | G 5[5\|4]4XXXXX A |
| | | U 26[1\|0]XXXXX A |
| | | ★ 368XXXX[1\|0] A |
| | 1957A | D 466[0\|1]XXXX A |
| | 1957B | U [3\|4]70XXXXX A |
| | | S 644XXX[34\|20] A |
| | | W 455[50\|18]XXX A |
| | | X 246XXXX[1\|0] A |
| | | ★ 977XXX[2\|0]X A |

| Denom | Type | Series | Serial Number[1] |
|---|---|---|
| $1 | FRN | 1963 | A XXXXX[112\|000] ★ |
| | | B 233XXX[0\|1]X A |
| | | B 574XXXX[0\|1] A |
| | | H 262XXXX[0\|8] A |
| | | H 8[7\|9]7XXXXX A |
| | | L 825XX[00\|11]X B |
| | 1969 | F 6[8\|7]9XXXXX A |
| | 1969A | D [4\|3]23XXXXX B |
| | 1969B | B 897XXXX[2\|0] C |
| | 1969D | B 76[0\|1]XXXXX C |
| | | B 4[4\|3]5XXXXX E |
| | | C 147X[00\|10]XXX B |
| | | G [0\|9]41XXXXX C |
| | 1974 | B 76[1\|0]XXXXX C |
| | | D 240[9\|0]XXXX A |
| | | D 888[0\|1]XXXX A |
| | | E 370X[0\|2]XXX D |
| | | E 7[5\|4]2XXXXX D |
| | | F 80[0\|1]XXXXX C |
| | | G 53[9\|0]XXXXX B |
| | | L 001[0\|1]XXXX D |
| | 1977 | B 66[6\|7]XXXXX F |
| | | E 022[0\|2]XXXX E |
| | | F 863XXXX[1\|0] A |
| | | F 976X[1\|0]XXX D |

| Denom \| Type | Series | Serial Number[1] |
|---|---|---|
| $1 \| FRN | 1977A | A [97250\|86139]XXXB[6] |
| | 1981 | A 994[1\|0]XXXX B |
| | | E 612XX[0\|1]XX B |
| | | F 5[22\|11]XXXXX E |
| | | F 9[9\|8]8XXXXX D |
| | | G 871X[1\|0]XXX B |
| | | J [4\|3]79XXXXX B |
| | 1981A | F 700[1\|0]XXXX B |
| | | F 9[8\|9]*XXXXX D |
| | | K 669[0\|1]XXXX B |
| | 1985 | E [0\|3]31XXXXX G |
| | | F [3\|2]18XXXXX G |
| | | L 893XX[1\|0]XX A |
| | 1988A | F 479XXX[0\|8]X H |
| | | G 259[0\|9]XXXX A |
| | | G [11\|00]0XXXXX ★ |
| | 1993 | F 784X[2\|1]XXX A |
| | 1995 | A 298X[1\|0]XXX A |
| | | D 581X[1\|0]XXX P |
| | | I [7370733\|0603065]X N[7] |
| | 1999 | A[1\|0]31XXXXX C |
| | | B XXXXX[00\|16]X J |
| | 2001 | B 764XX[58\|97]X B |
| | | I 98[5\|4]XXXXX A[8] |
| | 2003A | B 067XX[1\|0]XX F |
| | | B 711XX[0\|1]XX B |

| Denom \| Type | Series | Serial Number[1] |
|---|---|---|
| $2 \| FRN | 1976 | B 592XX[0\|1]XX A |
| | | F 700[1\|0]XXXX B |

| Denom \| Type | Series | Serial Number[1] |
|---|---|---|
| $5 \| NC | 1929 Type 1 | C 00[0\|1]001 A[9] |
| The Milliken NB of Decatur, IL. Charter #5089 | | |
| $5 \| US | 1928 | A 289XXXX[6\|0] A |
| | 1953 | A 100[0\|1]XXXX A |
| | | A 842XXX[1\|0]X A |
| $5 \| SC | 1934D | D XXXXX[579\|601] A |
| | 1953 | A 467X[1\|0]XXX A |
| | | A 477[0\|1]XXXX A |
| | | A 705XX[114\|000] A |
| $5 \| FRN | 1950 | G 815XXX[0\|1]X A |
| | 1950A | B 597XX[XXX\|700] C[10] |
| | | C 566XX[0\|1]XX A |
| | | E 648XXXX[0\|1] A |
| | | F 207XX[000\|108] B |
| | | H 403[0\|1]XXXX ★ |
| | | H [84\|48]2XXXXX A |
| | | J 262XXX[0\|1]X A |
| | | L 189XXXX[3\|0] B |
| | 1950B | I 376XXXX[0\|7] A |
| | 1950C | G 479XXX[3\|0]X D |
| | 1963A | E 6[4\|3]0XXXXX A |
| | 1969 | C 398XXX[11\|00] A |
| | 1969A | I 229[1\|0]XXXX A |
| | 1974 | I 61[1\|2]XXXXX A |
| | | J 3[6\|5]1XXXXX B |
| | 1977A | E 040X[1\|0]XXX ★ |
| | | H 673X[6122\|XXXX] A[11] |
| | | L 4[4\|5]5XXXXX B |
| | 1981 | B 4[4\|5]5XXXXX B |
| | 1985 | G 316X[7\|2]XXX B |
| | | G 585XXX[7\|0]X B |
| | 1988A | D 683X[0\|1]XXX B |
| | | L 294X[1\|0]XXX D |
| | 1995 | E 0[10\|01]XXXXX C |

| Denom \| Type | Series | Serial Number[1] |
|---|---|---|
| $10 \| NC | 1929 Type 1 | E 00[6\|5]207 A[9] |
| The Security NB of Pasadena, California. Charter #10167 | | |
| $10 \| SC | 1934 | ★ 0000000[5\|1] A |
|  | 1934D | D 776[0\|1]XXXX B |
| $10 \| FRN | 1928B | G [444460\|35208]XXX A |
|  | 1950 | A 085XXX[1\|0]X A |
|  |  | J 295[1\|0]XXXX A |
|  | 1950A | B XXXXXXX[[1\|0] C |
|  |  | D 956XXXX[1\|0] A |
|  |  | E 011[1\|0]XXXX ★ |
|  |  | F 358XX[66\|00] B |
|  |  | F 010XXX[0\|52] ★ |
|  | 1950B | C 076XX[1\|0]XX ★ |
|  | 1950D | D 573XXXX[0\|1] C |
|  |  | E 11[0\|1]XXXXX ★ |
|  | 1963A | E 6[3\|4]5XXXXX A |
|  | 1969 | E 393XXXX[9\|0] A |
|  | 1985 | I 102XXX[1\|0] A |
|  | 1990 | H363[9\|5]XXXX A |
|  | 1995 | I 125[1\|0]XXXX A |

| Denom \| Type | Series | Serial Number[1] |
|---|---|---|
| $20 \| GC | 1928 | A 010XXX[0\|1]X A |
| $20 \| NC | 1929 Type 1 | B 000[221\|187]A[9] |
| The First NB of Red Wing, Minnesota. Charter #1487. | | |
| $20 \| FRN | 1934 | F 003[1\|0]XXXX ★ |
|  | 1934A | G 006XXX[24\|01] ★ |
|  | 1950A | A 296XXXX[1\|0] A |
|  | 1950C | F 100XXXX[1\|0] B |
|  | 1977 | G 450[0\|1]XXXX B |
|  |  | L XXXXXX[63\|27] A |
|  | 1981A | B [1\|0]00XXXXX D |
|  | 1993 | J 005XX[3\|0]X A |
|  | 1996 | AL 786[0\|1]XXXX F |
|  | 2004 | ED 2[6\|7]XXXXXX C |

| Denom | Type | Series | Serial Number[1] |
|---|---|---|
| $50 | FRN | 1981 | D 054XXX[8|1]X A |

| Denom | Type | Series | Serial Number[1] |
|---|---|---|
| $100 | NC | 1929 | B00006[4|2]A[9] |
| The Winters NB & Trust Co. of Dayton, Ohio. Charter #2604. | | |

| Denom | Type | Series | Serial Number[1] |
|---|---|---|
| $100 | FRN | 1974 | L020XX[40|92]6★[10] |
| | 1985 | B05[8|9]XXXXXA |
| | 1996 | AB15[2|6]XXXXS |

| Denom | Type | Series | Serial Number[1] |
|---|---|---|
| $1000 | FRN | 1934 | H 000103[6|3]7 A[9] |

[1] - The Serial Numbers are listed with the mismatched digit(s) in brackets. The digits on the left side correspond to the left serial number, and the digits on the right side correspond to the right serial number. If the mismatch occurs in the first three digits used as the identifier, the digits in the brackets are the actual digits that will always be found on the note. If the mismatch occurs in the last five digits, one of the digits will be set to 0 and the other will correspond to digit that will occur when the other is 0. These digits can actually be any numbers but unless otherwise specified, the number of digits between the two will always remain constant.

*Example:* The listing A123XX[0|1]XA could have Serial Number A123XX0XA on the left and Serial Number A123XX1XA on the right. The [0|1] designator for the mismatched digit dictates that the right Serial Number digit is always 1 number greater than the corresponding left Serial Number digit on all known examples of this error.

[2] – This mismatch error is found in both sheet positions D & F. This is the only known mismatch to occur in more than one plate position on the half sheet.

[3] - The right Serial Number froze at *A 43611070 H* while the left Serial Number continued to advance.

[4] - Also known with differences of [9|0], [7|0], and [5|0].

[5] - This mismatch is also categorized as a Mismatched Prefix / Suffix error because the suffix of the left Serial Number is missing.

[6] - Also known with A [97251|86140]XXX B Mismatch. 1,200 of these notes were thought to be released into circulation.

[7] - The authenticity of this note is uncertain. It sold on an Internet Auction site in 2000.

[8] - This mismatch is found on uncut sheets of currency issued by the BEP with a single note having a mismatch. All single note examples of this error have been cut from sheets.

[9] - Actual Serial Number Listed. This note is thought to be unique.

[10] - The right Serial Number froze at *B 59707700 C* while the left Serial Number continued to advance.

[11] - The left Serial Number initially froze at *H 67356126 A* while the right Serial Number continued to advance (downward). The left Serial Number advanced several times as examples are also known with [6122|XXXX], [6123|XXXX] and [6125|XXXX] mismatches. There are no reported examples of a [6124|XXXX] mismatch.

[12] - Only known example is missing 15% of the right side of the note. Both Serial Numbers are intact.

**Additional Examples**

$1 LT Series 1862 – 8382[2|6] Mismatch

$1 SC Series 1899 – D 1150[6|7]050 A Mismatch

$1 USN Series 1869 – Z92034[67|71] ★ Mismatch

*Mismatched Serial Numbers - $1 SC Series 1957-B SC*
*S644  Mismatch – Rare Block*
**F - $350       XF - $750       CU - $1,250**

*Mismatched Serial Numbers - $1 SC Series 1957-B SC*
*U[3\4]70  Mismatc – Common Block*
**F - $250       XF - $500       CU - $750**

*Mismatched Serial Numbers - $1 FRN Series 1969 FRN*
*F6[8\7]9 Mismatch*
**F - $250       XF - $500       CU - $750**

*Mismatched Serial Numbers - $1 FRN Series 1969-B FRN*
*B879 Mismatch*

**F - $250**          **XF - $500**          **CU - $750**

*Mismatched Serial Numbers - $1 FRN Series 1977-A FRN*
*A[97250\86139] Mismatch*

**F - $500**          **XF - $1,000**          **CU - $2,500**

*Mismatched Serial Numbers - $1 FRN Series 1988-A FRN Star Note*
*G[11\00]4 Mismatch*

**F - $1,000**          **XF - $2,000**          **CU - $3,000**

*Mismatched Serial Numbers - $1 FRN Series 2001 FRN*
*B764 Mismatch*

**F - $250**        **XF - $500**        **CU - $750**

*Mismatched Serial Numbers - $1 FRN Series 2003-A FRN*
*B711 Mismatch*

**F - $250**        **XF - $500**        **CU - $750**

*Mismatched Serial Numbers - $2 FRN Series 1976 FRN*
*B592 Mismatch*

**F - $250**        **XF - $500**        **CU - $750**

*Mismatched Serial Numbers - $5 FRN Series 1950-A FRN*
*C566 Mismatch*

F - $500        XF - $1,000        CU - $1,500

*Mismatched Serial Numbers - $5 FRN Series 1974 FRN*
*J3[6\5]1 Mismatch*

F - $250        XF - $500        CU - $750

*Mismatched Serial Numbers - $5 FRN Series 1977-A FRN*
*H673 Mismatch*

F - $500        XF - $1,000        CU - $1,500

*Mismatched Serial Numbers - $5 FRN Series 1985 FRN*
*B879 Mismatch*

**F - $250**          **XF - $500**          **CU - $750**

*Mismatched Serial Numbers - $10 FRN Series 1950-A FRN Star Note*
*E011 Mismatch*

**F - $1,000**          **XF - $2,500**          **CU - $4,000**

*Mismatched Serial Numbers - $10 FRN Series 1963-A FRN*
*E6[3\4]5 Mismatch*

**F - $500**          **XF - $1,000**          **CU - $1,500**

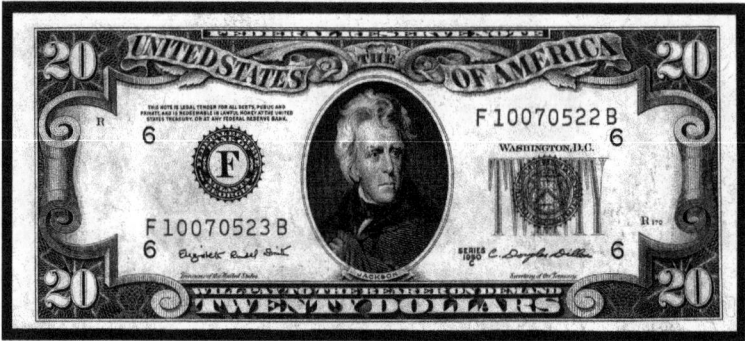

*Mismatched Serial Numbers - $20 FRN Series 1950-C FRN*
*F100 Mismatch*

F - $500                    XF - $1,000                    CU - $2,000

*Mismatched Serial Numbers - $20 FRN Series 1981-A FRN*
*B[1\0]00 Mismatch*

F - $500                    XF - $1,000                    CU - $2,000

*Mismatched Serial Numbers - $100 FRN Series 1974 FRN Star Note*
*L020 Mismatch*

F - $2,500                    XF - $5,000                    CU - $7,500

**Readers Notes**

# Mismatched Prefix / Suffix

Mismatched Prefix / Suffix Letters have a Class Rarity Rating of R8.

The Letters (and symbols) that are found before and after the serial numbers on US currency are called prefix and suffix letters. The initial use of the letters was as an anti-counterfeiting technique. Counterfeit notes bearing identical serial numbers were often quickly discovered. Counterfeiters started adding additional numbers to the serial numbers of their fake notes to make them appear different. 11 notes all bearing serial number 1234 could quickly become a single note with serial number 1234 and 10 notes with serial numbers ranging from 12340 to 12349. To stop this practice, the BEP began putting prefix letters and suffix symbols (a variety of symbols were used including a star on some series.)

Prefix letters on Federal Reserve Notes designate the Federal Reserve District Bank that will issue the note.

Prefix and suffix letters on modern currency are manually set with the serial numbers. These letters can be mismatched in the same manner as the serial numbers (see *Mismatched Serial Numbers* chapter).

## Large Sized Currency

No Mismatched Prefix / Suffix errors are known on Large Sized Currency.

## Mismatched Suffix Letters

**Known Examples**

| Denom \| Type | Series | Check Plate Position | Mismatch[1] |
|---|---|---|---|
| $1 \| SC | 1935E | | Y - [ ■ \|G][2] |
| $1 \| FRN | 1988A | 2 | F - [★\|L][3] |
| | 1995 | | [A\|K] – [C\|G][4] |
| | 1999 | C3 | C - [E\|I] |

[1] - The Serial Numbers are listed with the mismatched digit(s) in brackets. The digits on the left side correspond to the left serial number and the digits on the right side correspond to the right serial number. The listing C-[E/I] has Serial Number block C-E on the left and Serial Number block C-I on the right side.

[2] - This note has a solid rectangle on the left side and also has 4 digits in each serial number that do not match. It is more often classified as a Mismatched Serial Number error (See *Mismatched Serial Numbers* chapter)

[3] - This note is a web note (see Web Note Section in Paper Money Creation Overview chapter) and is also the only known mismatch of a star note and regular note. Serial Number F73056777[★\|L].

[4] – Mismatched Prefix and Suffix Letters. District Seal and letters suggest note was printed for Dallas (K) Federal Reserve Bank. Also listed in Mismatched Prefix listing.

## Mismatched Prefix Letters

### Known Examples

| Denom \| Type | Series | Check Plate Position | Mismatch[1] |
|---|---|---|---|
| $1 \| SC | 1957 | C3 | [A\|Q] - A |
| $1 \| FRN | 1969-B | | [C\|B] - C |
| | 1977-A | | [B\|A] - D |
| | 1981 | G3 | [A\|B] - H[2] |
| | 1988A | | [K\|L] - G |
| | 1995 | | [A\|K] – [C\|G][3] |
| | | H2 | [I\|-I] – E[4] |
| | | B2 | [-I\|I] – N[4] |
| | | | [J\|JZ] – Q[5] |
| | 1999 | | [K\|LK] – A[5] |
| | | C2 | [L\|-L] – W4 |
| $2 \| FRN | 1976 | H4 | [H\|B] - A |
| $5 \| SC | 1953-A | N | [D\|A] - A |
| $5 \| FRN | 1950-B | R | [D\|E] – B[6] |
| | 1981 | E4 | [J\|K] - A |
| | 2003A | | [FI\|FH] - A |
| $10 \| NC | 1929 Type 1 | G | [B\|A] – A[7] |
| Farmers & Merchants NB of Fort Branch, Indiana. Charter #9077. | | | |
| $10 \| NC | 1929 Type 1 | H | [B\|E] – A[8] |
| The First NB of Boston, Massachusetts. Charter #200. | | | |
| $10 \| FRN | 1981 | F4 | [I\|L] -★ |
| | | | [K\|L] - B |
| | 1981A | | [D\|E] - A |
| $20 \| FRN | 1996 | F1 | [AK\|AK - L] – A[9] |
| $50 \| FRN | 1977 | G4 | [A\|K] - ★ |
| $100 \| FRN | 1996 | | [AC\|AG] - A |

[1] - The Serial Numbers are listed with the mismatched digit(s) in brackets. The digits on the left side correspond to the left serial number and the digits on the right side correspond to the right serial number. The listing [A\|Q]-A has Serial Number block A-A on the left and Serial Number block Q-A on the right side.

[2] - This mismatch is found on uncut sheets of currency issued by the BEP with a single note having a mismatch. All single note examples of this error have been cut from sheets.

[3] – Mismatched Prefix and Suffix Letters. District Seal and letters are from Dallas (K). Also listed in Mismatched Prefix listing.

[4] – The dash before the Serial Number Prefix is often referred to as the 11th digit similar to those found on higher denomination currency. No $1 notes have been purposely printed with 11 digit serial numbers although examples exist with one of the prefixes displaying an extra digit.

[5] - This prefix of the right hand serial number has an extra letter in it.

[6] - This prefix "D" is a rolled digit with only the upper half of the letter showing. No portion of the "E" is visible.

[7] – Serial Number [B|A]000164A. Unique.

[8] – Serial Number [B|E]009643A. Unique.

[9] – Mismatched Prefix and Suffix Letters. District Seal and letters suggest note was printed for Dallas (K) Federal Reserve Bank. Also listed in Mismatched Prefix listing.

## Additional Examples

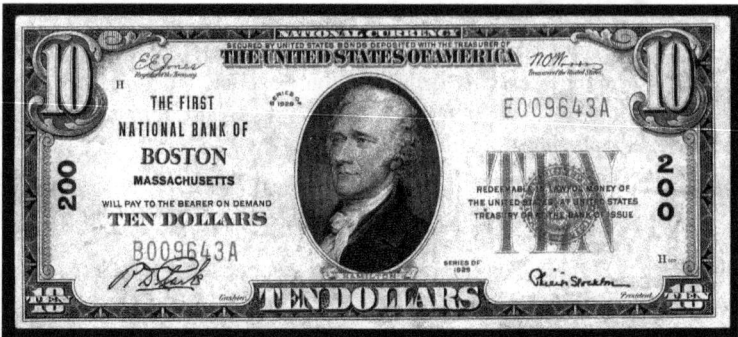

***[B | E] Mismatched Prefix Letters - $10 NC***
**F - $10,000          XF - $20,000          CU - $30,000**

***[B | A] Mismatched Prefix Letters - $10 NC***
**F - $10,000          XF - $20,000          CU - $30,000**

***[A | Q] Mismatched Prefix Letters - $1 SC***
**F - $500          XF - $750          CU - $1,000**

*[A | B] Mismatched Prefix Letters - $1 FRN – From Sheet*
F - $500        XF - $750        CU - $1,000

*[ ✴ | L] Mismatched Suffix Letters - $1 FRN Web Note*
F - $20,000      XF - $35,000      CU - $50,000

*[I | - I] Mismatched Prefix Letters - $1 FRN*
F - $1,000       XF - $1,500       CU - $2,000

*[E | I] Mismatched Suffix Letters - $1 FRN*
**F - $1,000          XF - $2,000          CU - $3,000**

*[L | - L] Mismatched Prefix Letters - $1 FRN*
**F - $1,000          XF - $1,500          CU - $2,000**

*[H | B] Mismatched Prefix Letters - $2 FRN*
**F - $250          XF - $500          CU - $750**

*[D | E] Mismatched Prefix Letters - $5 FRN*
**F - $500          XF - $1,000          CU - $1,500**

*[J | K] Mismatched Prefix Letters - $5 FRN*
**F - $1,000          XF - $1,500          CU - $3,000**

*[I | L] Mismatched Prefix Letters - $10 FRN Star*
**F - $2,000          XF - $4,000          CU - $8,000**

*[A | K] Mismatched Prefix Letters - $50 FRN Star*
**F - $3,000          XF - $6,000          CU - $9,000**

**Readers Notes**

# Mismatched
# Charter Nos.

In 1863, National Banks began to organize. These banks were issued official charters by the Comptroller of the Currency. A total of 14,348 National Banks were chartered between 1863 and 1935. The notes issued by these banks were required to display their charter number (the order in which their bank was chartered. Charter No. 1 for the first Bank and Charter No. 14348 for the last bank to be officially chartered by the US government) in multiple places on their faces (and backs of some notes). Over the years, these numbers were rubber-stamped, printed with the overprint and / or engraved on the face plates (and back plates of some notes).

**Known Examples**

| Denom \| Series | Charter | Serial No. |
|---|---|---|
| $5 \| 1902 DB | 3406 | 19988 \| B611695B |
| | | 20308 \| B612015B |
| The National Bank of Savannah, Georgia. Mismatched Charter Numbers in Overprint. Charter #3046 printed on left side and Charter #3406 (correct) printed on right side of note. | | |
| $5 \| 1929 Type 2 | 11978 | A001752 |
| | | A002332 |
| The First National Bank of Ashland, Virginia. Mismatched Charter Numbers. Charter #11878 is printed in brown ink near the serial numbers, but Charter #11978 (correct) is printed in black ink near the side margins of the face. | | |
| $5 \| 1902 DB | 1250 | A774749B \| 283007 |
| The Mechanics & Metals National Bank of the City of New York, New York. Mismatched Charter Numbers. Charter #3557 is printed on the face but Charter #1250 (correct) is printed along margins of face. | | |
| $10 \| 1929 Type 2 | 14150 | A001486 |
| First National Bank of Tigerton, Wisconsin. Mismatched Charter Numbers near Serial Numbers. Charter # 14150 (correct) printed on left side and Charter # 12150 printed on right side of note. | | |
| $10 \| 1902 DB | 10029 | 285 \| B239102A |
| The First National Bank of Bay Shore, New York. Mismatched Charter Numbers printed in blue near Serial Numbers. Charter # 10026 printed on left side and Charter # 10029 (correct) printed on right side of note. | | |

## Additional Examples

*Mismatched Charter 3046|3406*
**F - $15,000      XF - $20,000      CU -**

*Mismatched Charter 10026|10029*
**F - $15,000      XF - $20,000      CU -**

*Mismatched Charter 11878|11978*
**F - $10,000      XF - $15,000      CU -**

**Readers Notes**

# Incorrect Geographical Designator

To ease in the task of sorting redeemed National Currency, a geographical designator was added to the face of the notes.

The notes were separated into six district geographical regions.

| Designator | Region | States |
|:---:|:---|:---|
| E | Eastern | DC, DE, MD, NJ, NY, PA |
| M | Midwest | IA, IL, IN, MI, MN, MO, OH, WI |
| N | New England | CT, MA, ME, NH, RI, VT |
| P | Pacific | AK, AZ, CA, HI, ID, NV, OR, UT, WA |
| S | Southern | AL, AR, FL, GA, KY, LA, MS, NC, PR, SC, TN, TX, VA,WV |
| W | Western | CO, KS, MT, ND, NE, NM, OK, SD, WY |

These designators were printed on the face of the notes in two places.

These letters were part of the overprinting process and had to be setup by hand.

Although it is possible, there are no known examples of notes with mismatched geographical designators.

The known examples of incorrect geographical designators are on different denominations from the same bank.

**Known Examples**

| Denom \| Series | Charter | Serial No. |
|---|---|---|
| $10 \| 1902 RS | 884 | 1718 \| K248394[1] |
| First National Bank of Gardner, MA. Geographical Designator "M" (Midwest) printed on face instead of "N" (New England). | | |
| $20 \| 1902 RS | 884 | 1686 \| K248362 |
| First National Bank of Gardner, MA. Geographical Designator "M" (Midwest) printed on face instead of "N" (New England). | | |

1 – Incorrectly listed in some references as K284394. The 2 known examples are 32 serials numbers apart and were printed on 10-10-20-20 denominational sheets.

**$20 Note from the Same Bank as Known Examples of this Error.
Note has the Correct (N – New England) Geographical Designator.**

**Additional Examples**

*Incorrect Geographical Letters*
**F - $25,000       XF - $40,000      CU -**

**Readers Notes**

# Inverted
# Digits

Inverted Digits have a Class Rarity rating of R9.

The Serial Numbering wheels contain 10 digits (0 through 9). The prefix and suffix wheels have to be the same size and shape as the numbering wheels because they are attached together in the numbering blocks and work in conjunction with each other. This presented a problem because there are 25 possible letters (A through Z excluding O) that can be used for the suffixes (and prefixes of all types of notes except Federal Reserve Notes). The solution was to have open slots in these wheels that would allow any prefix or suffix block to be inserted into them.

Some of the numbering blocks in the COPE-PAK machines were designed to have more than one prefix wheel. This was in anticipation of a series exhausting all serial numbering possibilities (A0000 0001A through A9999 9999Z) and still requiring additional notes to be issued for that series. The intent (although this situation hasn't arisen yet) was to use multiple prefix letters for the next run (AA0000 0001A). This foresight enabled the COPE-PAK machines to be used for the overprinting of Series 1996 $100 notes (the first series to use multiple prefix letters).

The ability to place any prefix or suffix block in the open slots also allows the blocks to be placed in the slots upside down. Because the blocks are a mirror image of the letter to be printed, it is difficult to immediately identify some of the letters as being inverted.

Inverted Digits occur in one position on the overprinted sheet. The Inverted "W" error and the Series 1928 $100 FRN errors can be found on two check plate positions because the full sheets were cut in half prior to the overprinting process. The two Check Plate positions actually correspond to the same position on each half sheet.

## Large Sized Currency

**Known Examples**

| Denom \| Type | Series | Check Plate Position | Serial Number |
|---|---|---|---|
| $10 \| NC | 1902DB | B | 12623 |
| The First National Bank of Laramie, WY. Charter #4989. Inverted "8" in the right side Charter Number. | | | |
| $10 \| NC | 1902PB | C | 8520 |
| The Malta National Bank. Malta, Ohio. Charter #2052. Inverted "5" in the left side Charter Number. | | | |

## Inverted Digits on Modern Sized Notes

### Known Examples

| Denom \| Type | Series | Check Plate Position | Serial No. Block |
|---|---|---|---|
| $1 \| SC | 1935-E | | ★-D |
| Inverted Star in Left Serial Number. | | | |
| $1 \| SC | 1935-G | H | ★-G |
| Inverted Star in Left Serial Number. | | | |
| $1 \| SC | 1957 | E2 & E4 | M-A[1] |
| Inverted "W" in place of "M" prefix in Right Serial No. | | | |
| $10 \| FRN | 1950-B | | G - ★ |
| Inverted Star in Left Serial Number. | | | |
| $100 \| FRN | 1928 | D | K-★[2] |
| Inverted Star in Right Serial Number. | | | |
| $100 \| FRN | 1928 | F | K-★[2] |
| Inverted Stars in Both Serial Numbers. | | | |
| $100 \| FRN | 1928 | A & G | L-★[3] |
| Inverted Star in Both Serial Numbers. | | | |
| $100 \| FRN | 1928 | C & I | L-★[3] |
| Inverted Star in Right Serial Number. | | | |
| $100 \| FRN | 1928 | B & H | L-★[3] |
| Inverted Star in Left Serial Number. | | | |

[1] – Series 1957 $1 Silver Certificates from the M-A block had an upside down "W" used as the prefix during the overprinting process. This error is found in plate positions E2 and E4 (the same position on each half sheet.) Because there were multiple overprinting presses printing this run at the same time, not all M-A block notes from these 2 plate positions will display this error.

**Reported Examples of Series 1957 $1 SC with Inverted "W"**

| Serial No. | Grade | Plate Position |
|---|---|---|
| M 04098541 A |  | E2 |
| M 06658358 A |  | E2 |
| M 11772443 A |  | E2 |
| M 11774827 A | VF/XF | E2 |
| M 11774828 A | CU | E2 |
| M 14320484 A |  | E2 |
| M 19447824 A | CU | E2 |
| M 24259277 A | CU | E4 |
| M 25200518 A |  | E2 |
| M 25219429 A | F | E2 |
| M 33850844 A | XF | E4 |
| M 34804070 A |  | E4 |
| M 36402614 A |  | E4 |
| M 36413054 A |  | E4 |
| M 42816787 A |  | E4 |
| M 43765707 A | VF | E2 |
| M 47297791 A | VF | E4 |
| M 51773011 A | XF | E4 |

[2] – Series 1928 $100 FRN from the Dallas district has reported examples with the star in the right serial number inverted and with the stars in both serial numbers inverted.

**Reported Examples of Series 1928 $100 FRN Dallas Star Notes**

| Serial No. | Grade | Plate Position | Inverted Star Position |
|---|---|---|---|
| K 00001410 ★ | VF/XF | F | Both Serial Numbers. |
| K 00002208 ★ | F+ | F | Both Serial Numbers. |
| K 00002320 ★ | XF | D | Right Serial Number Only. |

The following table shows the status of the inverted stars in each Check Plate position.

| Series 1928 $100 FRN – Dallas District | | | |
|---|---|---|---|
| A | UNKNOWN | G | UNKNOWN |
| B | UNKNOWN | H | UNKNOWN |
| C | UNKNOWN | I | UNKNOWN |
| D | RIGHT | J | RIGHT |
| E | UNKNOWN | K | UNKNOWN |
| F | BOTH | L | BOTH |

[3] – Series 1928 $100 FRN from the San Fransisco district has reported examples with the star in the left serial number inverted, the star on the right serial number inverted and with the stars in both serial numbers inverted.

**Reported Examples of Series 1928 $100 FRN San Fransisco Star Notes**

| Serial No. | Grade | Plate Position | Inverted Star Position |
|---|---|---|---|
| L 00000073 ★ | CU | A | Both Serial Numbers. |
| L 00000181 ★ | CU | C | Right Serial Number Only. |
| L 00003593 ★ | AU | E | Both Serial Numbers. |
| L 00005261 ★ | VG | E | Both Serial Numbers. |
| L 00005837 ★ | XF | E | Both Serial Numbers. |
| L 00006112 ★ | VF | J | Neither. Both Stars Normal. |
| L 00006642 ★ | F | L | Neither. Both Stars Normal. |
| L 00007440 ★ | VF | L | Neither. Both Stars Normal. |
| L 00008396 ★ | F | H | Left Serial Number Only. |
| L 00010214 ★ | VG/F | H | Left Serial Number Only. |

The following table shows the status of the inverted stars in each Check Plate position.

| Series 1928 $100 FRN – Dallas District | | | |
|---|---|---|---|
| A | BOTH | G | BOTH |
| B | LEFT | H | LEFT |
| C | RIGHT | I | RIGHT |
| D | NONE | J | NONE |
| E | BOTH | K | BOTH |
| F | NONE | L | NONE |

## Additional Examples

**Inverted Star in Left Serial Number - $1 SC**
**F - $500          XF - $1,000          CU - $2,000**

**Inverted W in Right Serial Number - $1 SC**
**F - $500          XF - $1,500          CU - $2,000**

**Inverted Star in Left Serial Number - $10 FRN**
**F - $500          XF - $1,500          CU - $2,000**

**Inverted Star in Right Serial Number**
**$100 FRN Dallas District**
**F - $5,000          XF - $10,000          CU - $15,000**

*Inverted Star in Left Serial Number*
*$100 FRN San Fransisco District*
**F - $5,000        XF - $10,000      CU - $15,000**

*Inverted Star in Right Serial Number*
*$100 FRN San Fransisco District*
**F - $5,000        XF - $10,000      CU - $15,000**

*Inverted Star in Both Serial Numbers*
*$100 FRN San Fransisco District*
**F - $5,000        XF - $10,000      CU - $15,000**

*Inverted Digit in Charter Number -  $10 NC*
**F - $9,000        XF - $12,000      CU - $15,000**

**Readers Notes**

# Mismatched Block Fonts

Mismatched Block Fonts have a Class Rarity rating of R2.

During the production of $1 Federal Reserve Notes for Series 1969-B, 1969-C, 1969-D, 1974 and 1977, both the conventional overprinting presses and the COPE presses (see *Paper Money Creation Overview* chapter) were being used at the same time. Productions runs from nearly every district were intermixed between the different sets of overprinting equipment.

The appearance of the serial numbers on notes overprinted in the COPE presses is different than those overprinted in the conventional presses. On notes printed on the COPE press, the numbers (used for the prefix and suffix of the serial number) and the numbers are bolder. The most noticeable difference can be found on the letter "G".

**Serial Number Font Style for Conventional Overprinting**

**Serial Number Font Style for COPE Overprinting**

$1 Federal Reserve Notes overprinted with the COPE machine are known to exist with the proper prefix letter and the suffix letter meant o be used on the conventional overprinting machines.

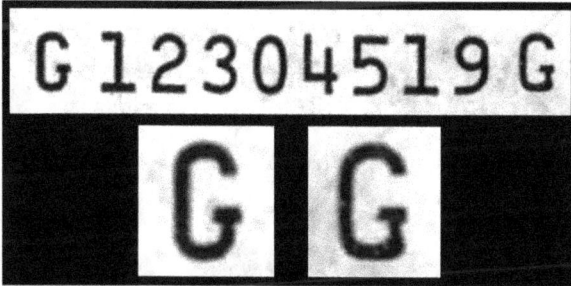

**Enlarged View of Mismatched Block Fonts**

**Known Blocks**

| Denom \| Type | Series | Block |
|---|---|---|
| $1 \| FRN | 1977 | B - G |
| | | G - G |
| | 1977-A | B - G |
| | | E - G |
| | | F - G |
| | | G - G |
| | | K - G |
| | | L - G |
| | 1981[1] | A - G |
| | | B - G |
| | | E - G |
| | | F - G |
| | | G - G |

1 – Although possible, this error has not been found on the L – G block.

**Additional Examples**

*Mismatched Block Font - $1 FRN Series 1977*
F - $5            XF - $10            CU - $20

*Mismatched Block Font - $1 FRN Series 1977-A*
F - $5            XF - $10            CU - $20

*Mismatched Block Font - $1 FRN Series 1981*
F - $5            XF - $10            CU - $20

**Readers Notes**

# District Designator Variance

Inverted Digits have a Class Rarity rating of R7

Series 1999 $20 FRN's have been discovered with a smaller sized District Designator. It is also positioned farther below the serial number than on a normal note. Unlike the minor differences in face plate size and positioning (see *Engraving Error* Chapter) this error is very noticeable.

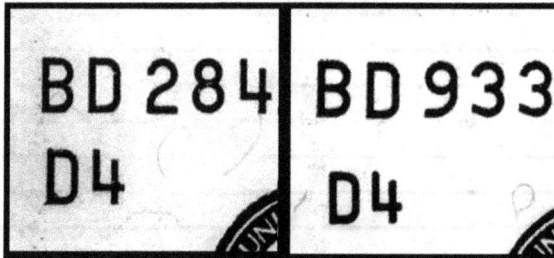

**Correct**
**3.5mm in Size**

**Error**
**3.0mm in Size**

**Confirmed Blocks**

| Denom | Type | Series | Block |
|--------------|--------|--------|
| $20 | FRN | 1999 | BD - A |
| | | BD - B |

**Additional Examples**

*District Designator Variance - $20 FRN Series 1999*
**F - $25          XF - $50          CU - $100**

**Readers Notes**

# Paper Problems

The paper used to create US currency is currently supplied exclusively by Crane Paper Company of Dalton Massachusetts. Crane has supplied paper for US currency since 1879. During this period of over 140 years of supplying paper to the worlds largest securities printer (the BEP), Crane has developed a set of internal quality control standards that ensure that the paper supplied to the BEP meets the stringent standards and requirements and that very few substandard sheets of paper escape the paper mill.

The currency paper provides a home for several anti-counterfeiting techniques. Small blue and red threads are embedded into the paper at the pulp (liquid) stage. The paper is also dyed a distinctive cream color while in this liquid stage. (Although premiums are attributed to some notes with *Creamier* paper, the different shades of paper that can be found are not considered errors.) Denominations of $5 to $100 currently have a plastic polymer thread running through them. The thread has the denomination and USA written across its length. Series 1996 and later have an anti-counterfeiting watermark embedded in the paper. The watermark is either a scaled down version of the portrait found on the face of the note or the denomination of the note. The security thread and the watermark are only visible when the note is held in front of a light source.

Paper Problems or Paper Errors are errors that are a result of something directly relating to the paper used for US currency. These problems have to do with the watermarks, security threads, the thickness of the paper, and splices and end of roll markers dyed into the paper. Unlike other paper related problems like folds (See *Folds and Tears* Section) and miscut notes (See *Cutting Errors* Section) that often occur within the BEP and can be caught by the inspectors, most Paper Problems are difficult to detect during the printing processes.

Most Paper Problems are very rare because of the quality control measures incorporated by Crane, but recent attempts by the BEP to qualify alternate paper suppliers will probably open the door to the discovery of many new paper problems when an alternate source is used.

# Misplaced Security Thread / Watermark

Denominations of $5 through $100 have a plastic polymer thread running through them (starting with Series 1990 $100 notes.) This thread has the denomination and USA written across its length. The new Series of currency (starting with Series 1996 $100 notes) has these threads in different positions on the notes to help identify notes that have been altered to be passed as a higher denomination ("bumped up"). New thread placements could give the collecting community some interesting errors as these threads get misplaced.

Series 1996 $100 notes are the first US notes to use a watermark as a security feature. This watermark is a scaled down version of the portrait found on the face of the note. Denominations $5 through $50 have also incorporated the watermark.

The watermark is in the process of being changed to the numeric denomination of the note.

When viewing a note with the security features from the face, the security thread is normally on the left hand side of the note and the watermark (on notes that have them) is on the right. Several errors have been discovered that have had the watermarks and / or security threads misplaced.

Errors involving notes that only have the security threads have the thread on the wrong side of the note.

Errors involving notes with both a security thread and a watermark have been found with both the watermark on the wrong side and on the wrong side and upside down.

When a Watermark is inverted, it will also be misaligned, splitting it so that portions of two different watermarks are visible on the face. This is because of the difference in the top and bottom margins of the full sheets prior to the trimming process.

In 1997, the BEP announced that approximately 1500 sheets of currency paper had been incorrectly marked at the paper mill. The positioning notch that identifies the top of the sheets was inadvertently placed on the bottom of the sheet and on the wrong side. When this paper was fed into the printing presses using this guide notch as an alignment aide, the watermark and the security thread were upside down and on the wrong side of the note. Out of the 46,000 notes known to be printed, 33,000 were discovered at the New York Federal Reserve Bank and were destroyed. The remaining notes were distributed to satellite banks in the New York Federal Reserve District.

Any of these notes that are returned to the Federal Reserve District will be destroyed. All notes from this run are overprint with serial numbers from the New York Federal Reserve District. Examples of this error from other districts are much rarer, but do not carry a pricing premium.

**Note has been Backlit so Security Features are Visible.
Security Thread is on the Right Side and
the Watermark is on the Left Side, Inverted,
Split so Portions of Two Different Watermarks are Visible.**

**Additional Examples**

*Security Thread on Right and Watermark on Left Side of Note*
*The Watermark on this Note is Inverted*
**F - $150          XF - $250          CU - $300**

*Security Thread on Right Side of Note - $20 FRN*
**F - $150          XF - $250          CU - $300**

*Security Thread on Right and Watermark on Left Side of Note*
*The Watermark on this Note is <u>Not</u> Inverted*
**F - $150          XF - $250          CU - $300**

*Security Thread On Right Side of Note - $100 FRN*
**F - $150          XF - $250          CU - $300**

*Security Thread on Right and Watermark on Left Side of Note*
*The Watermark on this Note is <u>Not</u> Inverted*
**F - $125          XF - $150          CU - $200**

*Security Thread on Right and Watermark on Left Side of Note*
*The Watermark on this Note is Inverted*
**F - $125          XF - $150          CU - $200**

## Readers Notes

# End of
# Roll Marker / Paper Splices

End of Roller Markers Splices have a Class Rarity Rating of R7.

Paper Splices have a Class Rarity Rating of R9.

The paper used in the production of US currency is processed into huge rolls at the paper mill. Several lengths of paper are spliced together in order to obtain a standard sized roll. These rolls will later be cut into the standard sized sheets of currency paper.

Electronic eyes scan the paper as it is being cut. These eyes are supposed to detect the splices that connect the different lengths of paper. These splices are cut out of the rolls so that they do not show up in the sheets meant for the currency. The scanners also detect markers that signify that the end of the current roll of paper is near. Rolls are marked with a dyed strip that runs the entire width of the roll. This strip is also supposed to be cut out of the paper and the cutting machine signals the operator to load a new roll for cutting.

Examples of notes with *Paper Splices* and *End of Roll Markers* have been discovered in circulation.

## End of Roll Markers

Notes have been discovered with red, purple and green strips dyed into the paper. Most modern note examples of this error have the strip visible on the right side of the face. The backs are almost always misaligned to the right. In fact, the backs are printed correctly, and the face print is misaligned so that the notes that are positioned along the right side of the sheet run into the end of roll strips that would normally get cut away during the trimming process. Once the notes are trimmed, the back printing appears to be misaligned.

A group of Series 1976 $2 notes have surfaced with the green strip on the left side and no misalignment of the back.

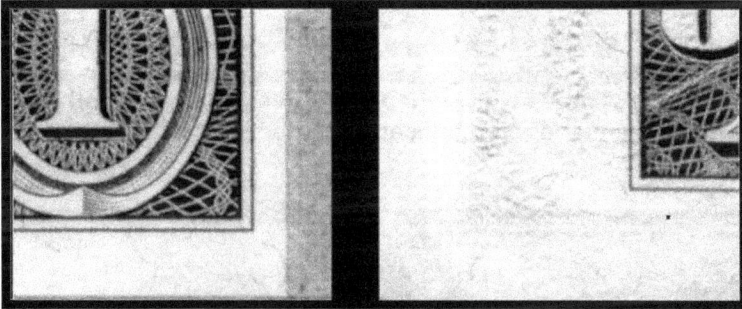

**Green Matte Strip Indicating End of Roll**
**Backs are Usually Misaligned**

**End of Roll Indicator on Early $1 Silver Certificate**
**The entire top edge of this note displays the red dye marker.**

## Paper Splices

Paper Splice errors are notes that have 2 sheets of paper overlap each other and are glued together. Modern examples of this error have a turquoise colored double sided tape strip holding the 2 pieces of paper together.

**Paper Splice – Two Overlapping Sheets Glued Together.**
**This Note was discovered spliced together but was later separated.**

**Separated Paper Splice - View From Front**

**Separated Paper Splice - View From Back**
**In its separated state, you can easily see Double Sided Tape.**

**Caution:** There have been some murmurs about "Failed Splice" errors where the two pieces are separated as in the example pictured above. These examples cannot be valued over that of a normal note, because separation is a fairly simple process. My example note was in a normal Paper Splice error when I bought it for the Taylor Family Collection, but it later surfaced as a "Rare Failed Splice."

**Additional Examples**

*Green "End of Roll" Marker Embedded into Paper*
*This note is Opposite of the Normal Error with the*
*Strip visible on the back and the misalignment on the face.*
**F - $500          XF - $1,000          CU - $1,500**

*Green "End of Roll" Marker Embedded into Paper*
*Visible on Left Edge of Face with No Misalignment*
**F - $250     XF - $500     CU - $1,000**

*Green "End of Roll" Marker Embedded into Paper*
*Normal (for Error Type) Misalignment of Back*
**F - $250      XF - $500      CU - $1,000**

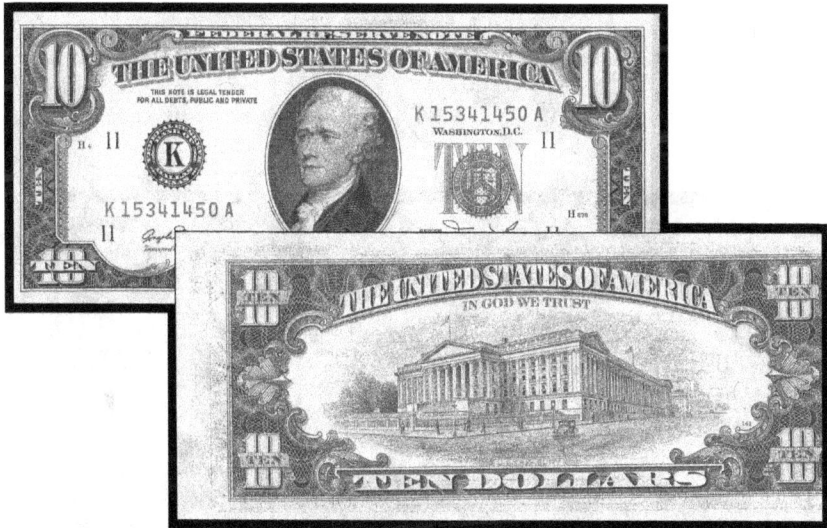

*Green "End of Roll" Marker Embedded into Paper*
*Normal (for Error Type) Misalignment of Back*
**F - $250      XF - $500      CU - $1,000**

*Paper Splice - $1 FRN*

**F - $750**       **XF - $1,500**       **CU - $2,500**

*Paper Splice - $10 FRN*

**F - $750**       **XF - $1,500**       **CU - $2,500**

*Paper Splice - $20 FRN*

**F - $750**       **XF - $1,500**       **CU - $2,500**

**Readers Notes**

# Thin / Thick Paper

Thin / Thick Paper has a Class Rarity rating of R9.

Currency paper is created by chemically treating a blend of cotton and linen under extreme heat and pressure. The liquid pulp that is created from this process is run through a variety of rollers that dry and roll the pulp into thinner and thinner sheets until it is the desired thickness. Improper adjustment of the rollers can create paper that is too thick or too thin.

There are no confirmed examples of "Thick Paper" errors. Previously reported examples of notes printed on paper that is too thick have proven to be paper slices or alterations.

**Additional Examples**

*$1 FRN with thin paper affecting the left side of the note*
**F - $150          XF - $300          CU - $600**

*$20 FRN with thin paper affecting the majority of the note*
**F - $200          XF - $400          CU - $800**

## Readers Notes

# Lamination Errors

Currency paper is **not** laminated in the sense that several thin layers of paper are bonded together but the method of rolling and pressing the pulp form of the paper into its standard thickness does allow the paper to dry in layers.

Although currency paper is fairly thin, it is possible for some of the different layers to peel away leaving the affected section of the sheet thinner.

**Author's Note:** While doing research for the first edition of this book, several examples of Lamination Errors were reported to me where a portion of the sheet peeled away after the face printing but prior to the overprinting process. Portions of the overprint were then printed on the thinner blank paper.

More in-depth research has found that these reported Lamination errors were actually Obstructed Print Errors.

**Currently, there are no confirmed examples of Lamination Errors.**

**Note:** Because it is possible to peel a note into two complete halves leaving the face printing on one layer and the back printing on another (often referred to as a Split Note), all examples of this are suspect and are **not** considered errors. Notes that have any portion peeled away but do not have one of the printings affecting the thinner section are also suspect.

# Readers Notes

# Process Errors

Process Errors are notes that do not follow the standard processes outlined in the *Paper Money Creation Overview* chapter.

Notes from this family include Double Denominations, Mixed Denominations, Wrong Overprints. and Test Note Errors.

# Double Denominations

Double Denomination Errors have a Class Rarity rating of R9.

A Double Denomination error is a note that has the face printing of one denomination and the back printing of another. This error is the ultimate process error and is often referred to as the "King of Errors" in the numismatic community (even though a few other error types are rarer with only a handful of examples known).

There are two distinct types of Double Denomination Errors. Double Denomination errors and Inverted Double Denominations. A Double Denomination error has its back and face in proper orientation with other although each is a different denomination. Inverted Double Denomination errors have their backs upside down in relationship to their faces.

Inverted Double Denomination errors occur only on National Currency. Many National Bank Notes were printed in multiple denomination sheets. When a sheet of these notes was turned around before the face printing, two different types of errors could be created. The notes that had the same denomination align are called Inverted Back errors. The notes that had different denominations align (usually the top an bottom notes of the sheet) were called Inverted Double Denominations. These notes have an inverted back but it is a different denomination than the face. Although the creation of this type of error is from an inverted sheet, these errors are categorized as double denominations (See *Inverted Back* Chapter). Many of the national notes had multi-colored backs. Only one color of the back has to be inverted for the note to be classified as an Inverted Double Denomination.

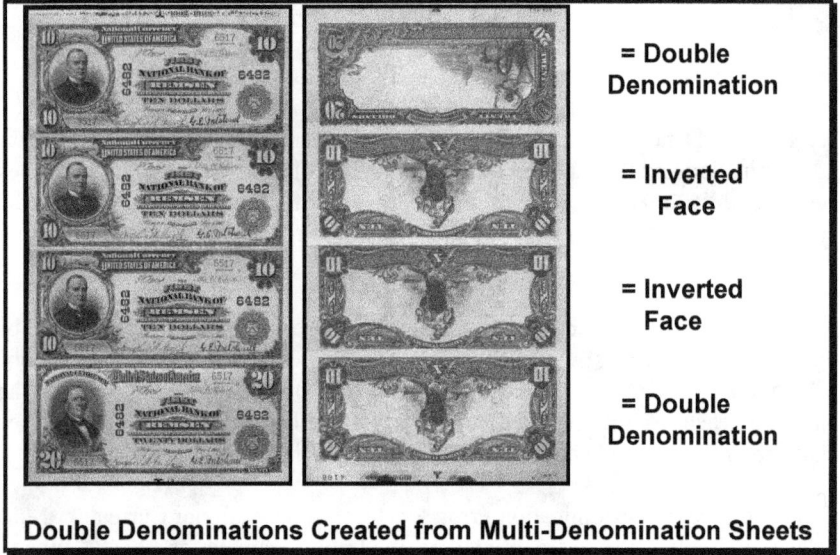

**Double Denominations Created from Multi-Denomination Sheets**

A variety of multiple denomination sheets combinations were used on National Bank Notes creating several different combinations of Inverted Double Denomination and Inverted Back notes printed from the same sheet (*See Inverted Back Chapter*).

**Large Sized Double Denomination – Non Inverted**

**Large Sized Double Denomination – Inverted**

## Large Sized Currency

Double Denomination Notes are the only error type of US Currency that is more plentiful on Large Sized Currency than on Small Sized Currency.

The following tables list the reported Double Denominations on Large Sized Currency.

**Large Sized $2 | $1 Double Denomination Notes:**

| Face | Back | Series | Fr No. | Grade | Serial No. |
|---|---|---|---|---|---|
| $2 \| $1 SC | 1899 | Fr 258 | VF | N68191165 |
| | | | VG | N68191166 |
| | | | CU | N68191167 |
| $2 \| $1 FRN | 1918 | Fr 747 | VF | A1831281A |
| | | | VG | A1831282A |
| | | | G/VG | A1831283A |
| | | | | A1831284A |
| | | Fr 751 | VF | B3140289A |
| | | | VG/F | B3140290A |
| | | | VF | B3140291A |
| | | Fr 765 | XF | G1302421A |
| | | | VG+ | G1302422A |
| | | | VG | G1302423A |
| | | | VF/XF | G1302445A |
| | | | F | G1302446A |
| | | | VF | G1302447A |
| | | | VF/XF | G1302448A |

**Large Sized $5 | $10 Double Denomination Notes:**

| Face | Back | Series | Fr No. | Grade | Serial No. |
|---|---|---|---|---|---|
| $5 \| $10 FRN | 1914 | Fr 868 | CU | G15011192A |
| | | | VG | G15011193A |
| | | | F+ | G15011195A |
| | | | XF | G15011196A |
| | | | XF | G18826673A |
| | | | F | G18826674A |
| | | | VF | G18826675A |
| | | | VF | G18826676A |

## Large Sized $10 | $20 Double Denomination Notes:
## National Currency

| Face / Back | Series | Fr No. | Grade | Serial No. |
|---|---|---|---|---|
| $10 / $20 NC | 2865 | Fr 409 | G/VG | Z970793 | 4515 |
| 2nd NB of Springfield, MA. Charter #181. | | | | |
| $10 / $20 DB | 1865 | Fr 412 | F | A459697 | 1491 |
| NB of Middlebury, VT. Charter #1195. | | | | |
| $10 / $20 DB² | 1882 | Fr 545 | F | R244989 | 1731 |
| 1st NB of Northport, NY. Charter #5936. | | | | |
| $10 / $20 VB² | 1882 | Fr 577 | CU | U109977 | 4899 |
| 1st NB of Barry, IL. Charter #5771. | | | | |
| $10 | $20 NC | 1882 | Fr 581 | VF | V95408 | 1620 |
| 1st NB of Smithton, PA. Charter #5311. | | | | |
| $10 / $20 VB | 1882 | Fr 577 | VF | U148693 | 138915 |
| Bank of Pittsburgh Nat. Assoc. Pittsburgh, PA. Charter #5225. | | | | |
| $10 / $20 VB² | 1882 | Fr 577 | CU | V162836 | 6128 |
| Citizens NB of Houghton, MI. Charter #5896. | | | | |
| $10 / $20 VB² | 1882 | Fr 577 | CU | V174210 | 17022 |
| Old Citizens NB of Zanesville, OH. Charter #5760. | | | | |
| $10 / $20 VB | 1882 | Fr 577 | AU | U368128 | 81244 |
| Lowry NB of Atlanta, GA. Charter #5318. | | | | |
| $10 / $20 NC² | 1902 | Fr 616 | CU | D177259B | 35251 |
| 2nd NB of Baltimore, MD. Charter #414. | | | | |
| $10 / $20 NC² | 1902 | Fr 618 | CU | E488983B | 10317 |
| American NB of Paris, TX. Charter #8542. | | | | |
| $10 / $20 NC | 1902 | Fr 619 | F | |
| Great Falls NB. Great Falls, MT. Charter #4541. | | | | |
| $10 / $20 NC | 1902 | Fr 623 | XF | M531888 | 190 |
| NB of Lumberton, NC. Charter #10610. | | | | |
| $10 / $20 NC | 1902 | Fr 623a | VF | |
| Northwestern NB of Grand Forks, ND. Charter #11142. | | | | |
| $10 / $20 NC² | 1902 | Fr 624 | XF | 2666 |
| 1st NB of Parkers Prairie, MN. Charter #6661. | | | | |

**Large Sized $20 | $10 Double Denomination Notes:**
**National Currency**

| Face / Back | Series | Fr No. | Grade | Serial No. |
|---|---|---|---|---|
| $20 / $10 NC[2] | 1882 | Fr 494 | XF | D984568 | 2475 |
| 1st NB of Washington, NJ. Charter #860. | | | | |
| $20 / $10 NC[2] | 1882 | Fr 555 | F | R550682 | 30968 |
| German NB of Cincinnati, OH. Charter #2524. | | | | |
| $20 / $10 NC[2] | 1882 | Fr 581 | CU | U109977 | 4899 |
| 1st NB of Barry, IL. Charter #5771. | | | | |
| $20 | $10 NC[2] | 1882 | Fr 581 | VF/X F | V95408 | 1620 |
| 1st NB of Smithton, PA. Charter #5311. | | | | |
| $20 / $10 NC | 1882 | Fr 581 | F | U148693 | 138915 |
| Bank of Pittsburgh Nat. Assoc. Pittsburgh, PA. Charter #5225. | | | | |
| $20 / $10 NC | 1882 | Fr 581 | AU | U367007 | 80123 |
| | | | XF | U368128 | 81244 |
| Lowry NB of Atlanta, GA. Charter #5318. | | | | |
| $20 / $10 NC[2] | 1882 | Fr 581 | CU | V174210 | 17022 |
| Old Citizens NB of Zanesville, OH. Charter #5760. | | | | |
| $20 / $10 NC[2] | 1902 | Fr 642 | AU | D177259B |35251 |
| 2nd NB of Baltimore, MD. Charter #414. | | | | |
| $20 / $10 NC | 1902 | Fr 642 | VF | D193087B | 34573 |
| Bank of North America. Philadelphia, PA. Charter #602. | | | | |
| $20 / $10 NC | 1902 | Fr 644 | VF | D702889B | 33767 |
| National City Bank of Chicago, IL. Charter #8532. | | | | |
| $20 / $10 NC[2] | 1902 | Fr 644 | CU | E488983B | 10317 |
| American NB of Paris, TX. Charter #8542. | | | | |
| $20 / $10 NC[2] | 1902 | Fr 650 | XF | 2666 |
| 1st NB of Parkers Prairie, MN. Charter #6661. | | | | |
| $20 / $10 NC | 1902 | Fr 649a | | |
| Northwestern NB of Grand Forks, ND. Charter #11142. | | | | |
| $20 / $10 NC | 1902 | Fr 653 | | 19664 |
| Great Falls NB. Great Falls, MT. Charter #4541. | | | | |

| Face / Back | Series | Fr No. | Grade | Serial No. |
|---|---|---|---|---|
| $20 \| $10 FRN | 1914 | Fr 964 | AU | A1851505A |
| | | | CU | A1851506A |
| | | | CU | A1851507A |
| | | | CU | A1851508A |
| $20 \| $10 FRN | 1914 | Fr 988 | CU | G10487345A |
| | | | CU | G10487346A |
| | | | CU | G10487347A |
| | | | CU | G10487348A |
| | | | F | G6710866A |
| | | | CU | G8811657A |
| | | | AU | G8811658A |
| | | | Ch AU | G8811659A |
| | | | AU | G8811660A |

**Large Sized $50 | $100 Double Denomination Notes**
National Currency

| Face \| Back | Series | Fr No. | Grade | Serial No. |
|---|---|---|---|---|
| $50 \|$100 NC[2] | 1882 | Fr 518 | CU | B592836 |
| 1st NB of Albuquerque, Terr. of New Mexico Charter #2614. | | | | |
| $50 \|$100 NC[2] | 1882 | Fr 559 | CU | A163737 |
| Columbia NB of Buffalo, NY. Charter #4741. | | | | |

**Large Sized $100 | $50 Double Denomination Notes**
National Currency

| Face \| Back | Series | Fr No. | Grade | Serial No. |
|---|---|---|---|---|
| $100 \| $50 NC[2] | 1882 | Fr 530 | CU | B592836 |
| 1st NB of Albuquerque, Terr. of New Mexico Charter #2614. | | | | |
| $100 \| $50 NC[2] | 1882 | Fr 567 | CU | A163737 |
| Columbia NB of Buffalo, NY. Charter #4741. | | | | |

[1] - AAG - Albert A. Grinnell sales of 1944 through 1947. This was the largest currency auction of its time and many rarities were cataloged without using the Serial Number in the description. Some of the notes from this sale have not yet resurfaced publicly.

[2] – Back is Inverted.

## Census of Known Small Sized Double Denominations:

**Small Sized $5 / $10 Double Denomination Notes:**

| Face / Back | Series | Fr No. | Serial No. |
|---|---|---|---|
| | | | J 43180723 A |
| | | | J 43180743 A |
| | | | J 43180744 A |
| | | | J 43180746 A |
| | | | J 43180748 A |
| | | | J 43180749 A |
| | | | J 43180750 A |
| | | | J 43180814 A |
| | | | J 43180815 A |
| | | | J 43180816 A |
| | | | J 43180817 A |
| | | | J 43180819 A |
| | | | J 43180820 A |
| | | | J 43180822 A |
| | | | J 43180823 A |
| | | | J 43180824 A |
| | | | J 43180826 A |
| | | | J 43180827 A |
| $5 \| $10 | 1934D | Fr 1960 | J 43180828 A |
| | | | J 43180829 A |
| | | | J 43312744 A |
| | | | J 43312749 A |
| | | | J 43312750 A |
| | | | J 43312751 A |
| | | | J 43312752 A |
| | | | J 43312813 A |
| | | | J 43312817 A |
| | | | J 43312818 A |
| | | | J 43312820 A |
| | | | J 43312821 A |
| | | | J 43312823 A |
| | | | J 43312824 A |
| | | | J 43312825A |
| | | | J 43312826 A |
| | | | J 43312827 A |
| | | | J 48180749 A |
| | | | J 54318017 A |

**Small Sized $10 / $1 Double Denomination Notes**

| Face / Back | Series | Fr No. | Serial No. |
|:---:|:---:|:---:|:---:|
| $10 / $1 | 1950A | Fr 2011 | B 52580340 D |
|  |  |  | B 52600340 D |
|  |  |  | B 52620340 D |
|  |  |  | B 52680340 D |
|  |  |  | B 52700340 D |
|  |  |  | B 52720340 D |
|  |  |  | B 52820340 D |
|  |  |  | B 52860340 D |

**Small Sized $10 / $5 Double Denomination Notes**

| Face / Back | Series | Fr No. | Serial No. |
|:---:|:---:|:---:|:---:|
| $10 / $5 | 1928A | Fr 2001 | E 04672279 A |
|  |  |  | E 04672280 A |
|  |  |  | E 04672281 A |
|  |  |  | E 04744279 A |
|  |  |  | E 04744280 A |
|  |  |  | E 04744281 A |
|  |  |  | E 04744282 A |
|  |  |  | E 04744284 A |

**Small Sized $20 / $10 Double Denomination Notes**

| Face / Back | Series | Fr No. | Serial No. |
|:---:|:---:|:---:|:---:|
| $20 / $10 | 1974 | Fr 2071 | K 46318252 B |
| | | | K 46318253 B |
| | | | K 46318254 B |
| | | | K 46338254 B |
| | | | K 46358252 B |
| | | | K 46358253 B |
| | | | K 46438254 B |
| | | | K 46438255 B |
| | | | K 46458252 B |
| | | | K 46458253 B |
| | | | K 46458254 B |
| | | | K 46658254 B |
| | | | K 46678151 B |
| | | | K 46678252 B |
| | | | K 46678254 B |
| | | | K 46696252 B |
| | | | K 46698252 B |
| | | | K 46698252 B |
| | | | K 46698254 B |

**New Double Denomination Possibilities**

**Security Thread and/or Watermark of Different Denomination:**

Security threads and embedded watermarks are being used on all denominations of US currency except the $1 and $2 notes. Each pallet of paper is marked with the denomination that is meant to be printed on it (matching the security thread if present) at the paper mill. Visual inspections are supposed to be performed at the paper mill and again at the BEP prior to the start of each printing run. Since different denominations of currency are often printed at the same time, it is feasible that a sheet (or multiple sheets) meant for one denomination could be printed as another denomination. This note would be classified as a Double Denomination error.

**Author's Note:** Although this error is possible, none have ever been confirmed.

A Series 1995 FRN from the Dallas district was discovered to have a small fragment of a security thread meant for the $10 denomination embedded in the paper.

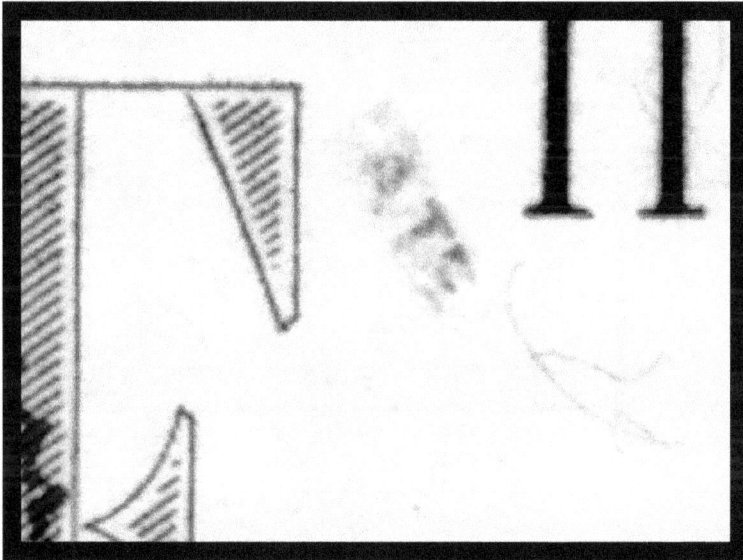

**Fragment of a Security Thread from a $10 FRN
embedded in the paper used to print this $1 Series FRN.**

While not a Double Denomination (the entire thread would be required), this error shows the possibilty of such an occurrence.

**Missing Security Thread**

It is possible for a denomination of currency meant to have a security thread and/or watermark ($5 - $100) to be printed on stock that was meant for $1 or $2 notes. These notes would lack the security thread and watermark.

**Author's Note:** These notes are rumored to exist but all 3 pieces I have examined have been altered. The security threads were pulled out of the notes and the gaps were glued together. One piece was highly convincing until it was held up to a light. The space where the thread had been was visible when backlit.

**Additional Examples**

*$10 | $5 Series Series 1928-A Double Denomination*
**F - $20,000    XF - $30,000        CU - $40,000**

*$5 | $10 Series 1934-D Double Denomination*
**F - $15,000    XF - $25,000        CU - $30,000**

*$10 | $1 Series 1950-A Double Denomination*
**F - $30,000    XF - $45,000        CU - $60,000**

*$20 | $10 Series 1974  Double Denomination*
**F - $20,000    XF - $30,000        CU - $40,000**

*$5 | $1 Series 1988-A  Double Denomination*
*The majorioty of the back design of a $1 Note can be clearly seen in a Large Ink Smear over the correctly printed $5 FRN Back*
**F - $10,000        XF - $15,000      CU - $25,000**

**Readers Notes**

# Mixed Denominations

Mixed Denomination errors have a Class Rarity Rating of R9.

A Mixed Denomination error occurs when a sheet (or sheets) of notes that has received the back and face printing of one denomination gets mixed in with a pallet of notes that were printed with the back and face printings of another denomination. When the notes receive their overprinting, the result is a set of notes from two different denominations with consecutive serial numbers.

**Caution:** Each set of theses error sets needs to be authenticated. It is possible to create a set of mixed denomination notes with consecutive serial numbers outside of the BEP. There are several examples of advertised sales of notes of different denominations bearing the same serial numbers. These notes are novelties and are put together from fresh packs of 100 notes taken directly from a bank that is furnished new money from a Federal Reserve Bank. It is time consuming but not difficult to create such a run of notes and if the same serial numbers can be pulled from these packs, logic dictates that consecutive notes can also be pulled from the same packs.

**Reported Examples**

| Denom \| Type | Date | Serial Number |
|---|---|---|
| $10 \| FRN | 1974 | E 01300024 C[1] |
| **$20 \| FRN** | 1974 | E 01300025 C |
| $10 \| FRN | 1974 | E 01300026 C |
| $2 \| FRN | 1976 | G 28949988 A[2] |
| **$20 \| FRN** | 1974 | G 28949989 A |
| $2 \| FRN | 1976 | G 28949990 A |
| $1 \| FRN | 1977 | A 88585910 A[3] |
| **$5 \| FRN** | 1977 | A 88585911 A |
| $20 \| FRN | 1990 | K 14174901 A[4] |
| $20 \| FRN | 1990 | K 14174902 A |
| $20 \| FRN | 1990 | K 14174903 A |
| $20 \| FRN | 1990 | K 14174904 A |
| **$50 \| FRN** | 1990 | K 14174905 A |
| **$50 \| FRN** | 1990 | K 14174906 A |
| **$50 \| FRN** | 1990 | K 14174907 A |
| **$50 \| FRN** | 1990 | K 14174908 A |
| $20 \| FRN | 1990 | K 14174909 A |
| $20 \| FRN | 1990 | K 14174910 A |
| $20 \| FRN | 1990 | K 14174911 A |
| $20 \| FRN | 1990 | K 14174912 A |
| $20 \| FRN | 1990 | K 18572098 A[5] |
| **$50 \| FRN** | 1990 | K 18572039 A |
| **$50 \| FRN** | 1990 | K 18572040 A |
| **$50 \| FRN** | 1990 | K 18572041 A |
| $20 \| FRN | 1990 | K 18572042 A |
| $20 \| FRN | 1996 | AA 24044644 A[6] |
| **$100 \| FRN** | 1996 | AA 24044645 A |
| **$100 \| FRN** | 1996 | AA 24044646 A |
| $20 \| FRN | 1996 | AA 24044647 A |

1 – Authentication: Series 1974 $20 notes printed for the Richmond (E) district started at Serial Number E 16640001 C. Serial Number E 01300025 C (the error) was printed for Series 1969C $20 notes.

2 – Authentication: The Overprint on the $20 is very high and would be considered a Moderate Misalignment if the note surfaced alone. This high overprint is in the same position that the overprints on the $2 notes appear (overprints on $2's are higher than any other denomination).

3 – Authentication: This set was reported before the Series 1977 $5 notes reached the 30 million mark in production (A 30000000 A).

4 – Authentication: The overprinting (particularly the green Treasury Seal) is markedly lower on the $50 denomination. It is in alignment with the seal of the $20 denomination.

This is one of two Mixed Denomination Set of $20 | $50 from Series 1990 and from the Dallas district. This set contains four $50 notes.

5 – Authentication: The overprinting (particularly the green Treasury Seal) is markedly lower on the $50 denomination. It is in alignment with the seal of the $20 denomination.

This is one of two Mixed Denomination Set of $20 | $50 from Series 1990 and from the Dallas district. This set contains three $50 notes.

6 – Authentication: The Universal Seal of the $20 notes is printed ontop of the Seal of the $100 note.

**Additional Examples**

*$20 | $50 Mixed Denomination Set*

F -                    XF - $6,000        CU - $12,000

*$20 | $100 Mixed Denomination Set*

F -                    XF - $10,000        CU - $20,000

**Readers Notes**

# Wrong Overprint

Wrong Overprint Errors have a Class Rarity Rating of R9.

Each Type of modern US currency has an overprint that is easily distinguishable from the other types. United States Notes have a red overprint, National Currency have a brown and black overprint, Silver Certificates have a blue and black overprint (some emergency war issues had brown and yellow seals), Gold Certificates have a gold overprint and Federal Reserve Notes have a green and black overprint.

Federal Reserve Notes are the only type of currency being printed today, but there have been numerous occasions when multiple types of currency were being printed in the BEP at the same time. There are two recorded cases where a sheet of notes printed for one type of currency were accidentally overprinted with the Seals and Serial Numbers meant for another type of currency. Only three examples from these two sheets (of 18 notes) are known to have survived.

The newest examples of the Wrong overprint error are Series 1988A Web notes that were printed as replacement (star) notes for the Atlanta (F) District. The BEP announced that no Star Notes would be printed on the Web fed notes and almost immediately after the release of this information, examples began to appear in circulation. There are thousands of examples of this error in various grades but because of the publicity, many were saved in Uncirculated condition.

**New Wrong Overprint Possibilities**

**New Series Overprints on Higher Denonations**

The overprints on $1 and $2 denominations currently being printed are different from that of $5 though $100 denominations. They are easily distinquishable by the placement of the serial numbers, the difference in the District (or Universal) Seals and District Letter designator and the number of letters in the prefix of the serial number.

It is possible for $1 or $2 notes to be mistakenly given the overprint meant for higher denomination notes or $5 through $100 notes to be overprinted as if they were lower denomination notes.

**Author's Note:** Although this error is possible, none have ever been confirmed.

**Reported Examples**

| Denom. / Type | Series | Serial Number |
|---|---|---|
| $5 / FRN | 1950 | A 11567022 A |
| $5 / FRN | 1950 | A 11599022 A |
| These Federal Reserve Notes have the blue overprint meant for Silver Certificates. | | |
| $5 / FRN | 1953B | C 45126235 A |
| This Federal Reserve Note has the red overprint meant for US notes (Legal Tender). | | |
| $1 / FRN Web | 1988A | F-★[1] |
| Replacement (Star) notes were not supposed to be printed for the Web Fed Experimental notes. Shortly after the BEP issued a Press statement that no Star Notes would be printed on the Web Notes, these errors began to appear in circulation. The BEP speculates that a pallet of Web Notes was inadvertently sent through the overprinting process (setup for a run of Star Notes) that was meant for a regular issue of notes. | | |

[1] - It has been argued that these notes are not true errors because the 1988A Web notes are Federal Reserve Notes and some Federal Reserve notes were supposed to be printed as replacement notes. These notes, however, are true Process errors. They went through a printing process that was not meant for them. There is no record of their printing in the BEP. While they are not nearly as rare as the other known examples of this error, they are errors and are worthy of any advanced error note collection.

## Additional Examples

*Federal Reserve Note with Red Overprint of a US Note*
**F - $35,000        XF - $50,000        CU -**

*Web Note with Replacement (Star) Note Overprint*
**F - $600        XF - $900        CU - $1,200**

**Readers Notes**

# Test Note Errors

Test Note Errors has a Class Rarity Rating of R9.

At the startup of a printing press, the plates are flooded with ink to test the press. After the tests, the sheets used are destroyed.

A small sampling of these notes has received the proper face, back and overprinting and have found their way into circulation.

**Additional Examples**

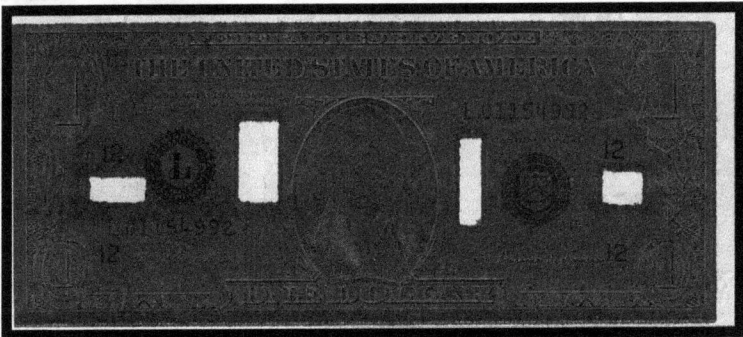

*Printing Press Test Note – Face - $1 FRN Star (Unique)*
*Voids are Non-Inked Areas Used for Additional Securiy Features*
**F -                    XF - $15,000     CU - $20,000**

*Printing Press Test Note - Back - $20 FRN*
**F -                    XF - $1,000      CU - $1,500**

**Readers Notes**

# Obstructed Plate

Obstructed Plate Error have a Class Rarity Rating of R9.

Sometimes foreign objects fall between the printing plate and the sheet of currency stock. Notes have been found where the foreign object has caused the raised area to be inked, allowing the object to be identified.

**Known Examples**

| Denom | Type | Series | Serial Number |
|---|---|---|
| $5 | FRN | 1974 | L34818918D |
| | | L34818922D |
| Paper Clip between Currency Sheet and Impression Cylinder. Raised impression of the paper clip has been inked, as if part of the face plate design. | | |

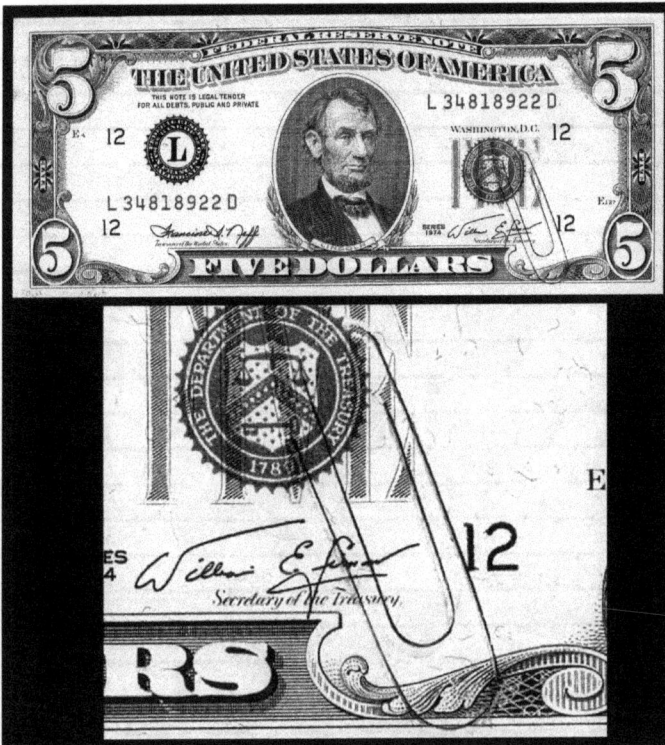

*Impression of Paper Clip Printed on Face of Note*
F -       XF - $2,500       CU - $5,000

**Readers Notes**

# Pre-Printed Stock

Pre-Printed Stock Errors have a Class Rarity Rating of R9.

Pre-printed Stock errors are created when currency is printed on paper that has a non-currency related printing already on it.

**Known Examples**

| Denom. | Type | Series | Serial Number |
|---|---|---|
| $20 | FRN | 1969-C | F 70145425 A |

There is a chevron pattern imprinted under the face and overprinting.

| $20 | FRN | 1995 | D 49103475 A |

Several small black cirles are printed under the face and back designs. This note also has the overprint on the back.

| $20 | FRN | 1996 | AL 34664829 B |

There is a mirror imaged, inverted bar code printed under thae face and overprinting.

**Additional Examples**

*$20 FRN with Barcode Printed under the Face and Overprint*
**F - $2,000      XF - $4,000      CU - $6,000**

**Readers Notes**

# Printed
# Scrap / Fragments

Printed Scrap has a Class Rarity Rating of R9.

Printed Scrap Errors are fragments of paper that have received a portion or portions of any of the currency printing process. These fragments can be currency stock or any other type of paper.

The floor of the BEP is littered with pieces of currency stock that were trimmed from the margins of full sheets, and with pieces of mutilated currency that were jammed and later cleared from the printing presses.

Very rarely, one of these pieces gets attached to a normal sheet of currency and picks up some of the printing process it is receiving. The scrap later makes it through the entire currency creation process and escapes the BEP in a pack of new currency.

These scraps can also be created when a normal sheet of currency gets jammed in one of the presses and get wrinkled, torn or mutilated.

**Additional Examples**

*Fragment of Currency Stock*
*Mutilated During Overprinting*
**$2,000**

*Fragment of Currency Stock*
*Portions of Two Overprints are Printed on the back*
**$2,000**

*Fragment of Currency Stock*
*No Overprinting is Visible*
*Note the Unprinted Folds at Lower Right of Face*
*$2,000*

**Readers Notes**

# Multiple Errors
# on Same Note

A Multiple Error is a note that displays two or more different errors. The errors must be different or affect different printing processes. Multiple Ink Smears on the back of a note would not be considered a Multiple Error, but an Ink Smear on the back and an Ink Smear on the Face of the same note would. Multiple Errors are very rare and nearly every one is unique.

Several Errors are incorrectly classified as Multiple Errors. The following list describes some of the Errors that are often mistaken for Multiple Errors

**Misaligned Face:** A Misaligned Face error with a correctly position overprint (positioned to the cut of the note) is often described as having the overprint shifted as well (See *Misaligned Face / Back* Chapter).

**Inverted Back:** An Inverted Back error on a Series after 1977A is often described as being miscut as well because a large portion of the note below shows on the back (See *Inverted Overprint* Chapter).

**Inverted Overprint:** An Inverted Overprint error on a Series after 1977A is often described as being miscut as well because a portion of the note above shows on the face (See *Inverted Overprint* Chapter).

**Inverted Overprint on Back:** The Inverted Overprint on Back error has been described as a Multiple Error because it appears to be a combination of an Inverted Overprint and an Overprint on Back error (See *Inverted Overprint on Back* Chapter).

**Gutter Fold and Cutting Error:** Gutter folds that remain closed during the cutting operations will usually displace portions of the design and the paper when they are opened. The larger the fold, the more paper is displaced. This is not a true cutting error. It is part of the Gutter Fold error itself (See *Gutter Folds* Chapter).

# COMPARATIVE CRIMINOLOGY
# A TEXT BOOK

## Part One

by

### HERMANN MANNHEIM

Routledge
Taylor & Francis Group
LONDON AND NEW YORK

First published in 1965
by Routledge

Reprinted in 1998, 2001, 2002
by Routledge
2 Park Square, Milton Park, Abingdon, Oxon, OX14 4RN
711 Third Avenue, New York, NY 10017
Transferred to Digital Printing 2007

*Routledge is an imprint of the Taylor & Francis Group*
First issued in paperback 2013
© 1965 Hermann Mannheim

*British Library Cataloguing in Publication Data*
A CIP catalogue record for this book
is available from the British Library

ISBN13: 978-0-415-17731-3 (hbk)
ISBN13: 978-0-415-84671-4 (pbk)

**Publisher's Note**
The publisher has gone to great lengths to ensure the quality
of this reprint but points out that some imperfections
in the original may be apparent

**Printed Fold with Additional Obstruction:** Printed Folds that opened prior to the cutting process are often misclassified as a multiple error because the unprinted portion of the note is a different size than the fold. It is often labeled as "an additional obstruction" causing the extra missing print when it was only the extra margins that were trimmed during cutting (See *Folds Affecting Prints* Chapter).

**Thumb Print on Back with other Error:** Many notes are advertised as having a *thumb print* in the center of their back. This print is usually a minor offset of a portion of the portrait from the face of the note directly beneath it. The inked lines that make up the contour of the face engraving and give it a three dimensional appearance are raised and often transfer (slightly) wet ink to the next sheet.

**Author's Note: Every** example that I have examined has turned out to be the offset described above, however, true examples of this error may exist. Hold the face of a similar note next to the thumb print in question and look for similarities in the patterns. A real thumb print should be easily recognizable when compared to the etched lines of the portrait.

**Additional Examples**

*Misaligned Overprint and Misaligned & Skewed Back*
**F - $250      XF - $500      CU - $1,000**

*Misaligned Face and Obstructed Print on Face*
**F - $125          XF - $250          CU - $5,000**

**Readers Notes**

# About
# the Author

Stephen M. Sullivan has always been a collector at heart. At the age of six, he found an 1899 Indian Head Penny under his front porch. His fascination with the strange-looking coin led to a trip to the local library where the few books on coins fueled his collecting interests. Soon, the hobby became an addiction, and with the help of several family members, his collection began to grow. By age ten, he decided to specialize in Silver Dollars, the coin he had the most examples of. It took another ten years to complete a collection of silver dollars (in XF and above) with a specimen from every issuing year from 1878.

At twenty years old, he sold his silver dollar collection and switched his specialty to paper money ($1 notes, of course.) It took another twelve years to complete this collection (with the purchase of a $1 Silver Certificate Series 1928-E star note that had been burned over 20% of its surface.) This collection also gave birth to the $1 Error Note Collection and his fascination with printing errors on modern U.S. currency.

Over the years, he has also collected Stamps, Matchbook Covers, Beer Cans (including several error cans), Playboy magazine covers (boasting a December 1953 Marilyn Monroe cover), Sports Cards, Bank Histories, Dinosaur Droppings (not a joke), and carnivore skulls.

www.ingramcontent.com/pod-product-compliance
Lightning Source LLC
Chambersburg PA
CBHW050557270326
41926CB00012B/2086